GERALD KENNEDY, Bishop of the Los Angeles Area of the Methodist Church, is one of today's best-known preachers and writers. Consecrated bishop at the age of 40, he is still the youngest bishop in his denomination. Much earlier than this however he was writing books; this is his twelfth. Among his most popular: HIS WORD THROUGH PREACHING, HAVE THIS MIND, THE LION AND THE LAMB, WITH SINGLENESS OF HEART, GO INQUIRE OF THE LORD, A READER'S NOTEBOOK and WHO SPEAKS FOR GOD?

In addition to his church work and lecturing, Bishop Kennedy finds time to do considerable book reviewing, both printed and over radio and TV.

No. 5533A

GOD'S GOOD NEWS

Gerald Kennedy

GOD'S GOOD NEWS

. . . set apart to declare God's good news . . .
ROMANS 1:1 (*Goodspeed*)

Harper & Brothers, Publishers, New York

FIRST EDITION B-E

Library of Congress catalog card number: 54-11662

THIS IS FOR MARY

CONTENTS

PREFACE

The December day which brought me an invitation to deliver the Lyman Beecher Lectures at Yale Divinity School one year and five months hence, is not likely to be forgotten. The honor was so great and so unexpected that I had to tell someone immediately or burst with pride. I called my wife and she managed to calm me down.

But time never sped so swiftly as during the next year. You may remember the fellow who said that if time is dragging, sign a ninety-day note. Before I knew it, the occasion was upon me and the lectures had to be delivered. The closer the day approached, the more grievous was the burden and the more fearful was my heart. It came to me again that for every ounce of honor in this life, there is a pound of responsibility.

The welcome from Dean Liston Pope, the members of the faculty and student body, and from the ministers of all denominations who attended the lectures, set me at ease. I cannot refrain from expressing my thanks to my predecessor in the Lectureship, Dr. Halford E. Luccock. His sympathetic encouragement did much to make the week memorable for me. Along with the New England springtime, these fine friends filled the days with sunshine and beauty.

I did my best to keep from bringing dishonor to a great tradition. As usual, my reach exceeded my grasp and it is a personal regret that my best is not better. I take some poor comfort that my brethren think of me as a preacher rather than as an administrator, or a writer. Thus be it ever! Preaching is the supreme calling and the greatest joy. May preachers young and old know this and never doubt it.

GERALD KENNEDY

Hollywood, California

GOD'S GOOD NEWS

I *Good News of God*

> Be not afraid; for behold, I bring you good news of a great joy which will come to all the people. . . .
>
> LUKE 2:10[1]

Some years ago an inquiry was made of a Methodist bishop regarding a preacher in his Area. "Why," said the bishop, "he is dull. He is supernaturally dull"; and then he added, "No man could be as dull as he is without divine aid." While it is not true, fortunately, that many men deserve this extreme judgment, still it is true that there are far too many of us who proclaim the Gospel without a proper sense of its excitement. Because it has lost its dramatic interest for us, we fail to give the good news any dramatic power when we tell other people about it. Spurgeon referred to one of his contemporaries as a preacher who would make a very good martyr; he was so dry he would burn well. It is a sad truth that for many people of our time, the noun "sermon" and the adjective "dull" are synonymous.

The place where we go wrong is the assumption that

[1] Unless otherwise noted Biblical references are to *The Holy Bible, Revised Standard Version,* Nelson, 1952.

preaching is editorializing or giving advice. Not so! It is headline stuff blaring forth the news about a Man, a Life, a Way, an Answer. It is never monotonous, for just when it seems all terror and judgment, it lights up with a testimony of God's graciousness and the gentleness of His commands. And whether the preacher's mood is dark or bright (and it will never be one or the other constantly) still there is beneath it an underflow of shouting and hallelujah. Preaching is not going from door to door to sell a book on home remedies, but standing on a street corner shouting "Extra!"

On the other hand, there is a kind of preaching which endeavors to escape dullness and becomes merely trivial and sentimental. It is a kind of shallow commentary which never dares to face the real tragedies of life. Thus some time ago a man wrote a letter to the *Saturday Review* and complained because an article had intimated that the supreme need of today was the Christian religion. He said Christianity was too tender for these tough times. One wonders what kind of preaching that brother had been sitting under to gain the impression that there is no toughness in Christianity. Had he never been told about the martyrs, the saints and the apostles? Had he never learned anything about church history? It is really no solution to the problem of dullness if a preacher succeeds in becoming merely a shallow sentimentalist. We will do well to remember a line in John Wesley's preface to his collection of hymns: "Here is nothing turgid or bombast, on the one hand, or low and creeping, on the other."

In the middle of the last century, a Methodist missionary arrived in San Francisco. There in the midst of the feverish excitement of the gold rush, William Taylor discovered there was no church for him to preach in and no congregation very much interested in listening to him. But on the streets of the city there were people from all over the world, and that was enough for him. Standing on a barrel at a busy corner on Sunday morning, he would gather a crowd about him with a mighty shout, "What's the news?" Then when they gathered to hear what this strange fellow had to say, he would begin his preaching with these words: "Thank God, I have good news for you this morning, my brothers." It is in that mood that every preacher should stand in his pulpit on the Sabbath to proclaim his message. We must never forget that the Gospel means "good news." It is not the recitation of laws and regulations, nor is it the placing of a more grievous burden upon the backs of sinners. It is not a sentimental word of sweetness and light which ignores hope gone sour and darkness too black to penetrate. For whether we are speaking of mercy or judgment, we approach every theme from the experience of God's love. To every man within the sound of our voice, no matter what his condition may be, we are the bearers of the tidings of great joy.

1. PERSONALITY

And he said to them, "The sabbath was made for man, not man for the sabbath. . . ." MARK 2:27

If there is one thing clear in the life and teachings of Jesus, it is his constant insistence that nothing must be considered more important than men. No institution, whether it be religious or political, is to be preferred above humanity. His most bitter denunciations were against the Pharisees, because their moral pride in the Law had blinded them to the needs of ordinary men. To turn our backs upon our fellows in the name of a higher obligation to some code or organization was in his thinking like turning our backs upon God. When the final judgment comes and when all of the truth about men is laid bare, then, said Jesus, the whole decision will rest upon the measure of their compassion and sympathy. The ultimate sin for any man is to be in the world of persons with claims upon him and deny them.

One of the popular misapprehensions of our time is an assumption that Christianity is to be equated with some particular political organization or some specific economic system. It is, I suppose, a manifestation of the fundamental sin of pride which tries to identify God with ourselves and our own institutions. The sin is particularly manifest today when an enemy challenges our assumptions and our values. It is well for us to remember that from the beginning of Christianity there have been Christians in all kinds of societies, living under all kinds of political systems. There is no reason to believe that this is going to change in the foreseeable future. Men will live in democracies and they will live under dictatorships; there will be Christians in both systems. The church will have to function in capitalistic societies, in socialistic societies, as well as under dictatorships. While it comes as a great shock to many people, the truth is that behind the iron curtain there are millions of witnessing Christians.

We can see how the temptation works with us. We begin by saying that Christianity is to be equated with democracy. Nobody argues about that if we say it in America, for the term is general enough anyway to cause little difficulty. Encouraged by this, we go a step further and say that Christianity is to be thought of as another word for American democracy. And again, if we speak only to America, we will find very little objection to this definition. Now go a step further and suggest that Christianity is to be thought of as a particular party's interpretation of American democracy.

This causes a little more lifting of eyebrows and perhaps vigorous dissent here and there. But we can take care of this by suggesting that our critics are un-American. The final step is taken when we decide that Christianity is really the Smith part of the party, or the Jones part, according to our taste.

There is not much exaggeration in this outline. Most of us in the ministry have talked with people within recent days who have insisted in all seriousness that the Christian Gospel is as simple as that. It is simply their particular economic and political point of view, tinged with some emotion, and perhaps flavored now and then with a religious vocabulary. There are people in our own country who would make the American church nothing more than a morale builder for the nation. Some wag defined the Church of England as the Tory party at prayer. Always there are with us those persons who want to make Christianity the sole possession and monopoly of a certain class with a particular point of view.

Now when we deny that this is possible, it does not mean that Christianity has no concern about political parties or economic systems. It has, as a matter of fact, a very great concern for everything that has to do with human life. It always comes to ask specific, pointed, embarrassing questions of every government and every social organism. An old man, walking down the street one day, saw a small boy looking after a baby. "Son," he asked, "what is your little brother's name?" The boy looked up and said, "If he were my brother his name might be Jack, but he ain't, and her name is Ruth." When men ask the wrong questions, they get the wrong answers, and one of the Gospel's great services is to help men ask the right questions about their institutions.

Christianity always asks what a system does to people. It assumes that persons are of final value and it will not be prevented from making an inquiry as to how men fare within the framework of a particular social organization. The Gospel is not interested primarily in labels and it is not overly impressed by verbal claims. It wants to know what the status of women is in this particular situation, and what happens to children. It insists on an answer to the question of whether men are recognized as ultimate ends and given a chance to claim their status as sons of God. Often it comes, therefore, as a judgment and a consuming fire; for it comes to proclaim the good news that in this universe persons are of essential significance, and God weighs all our social life against that balance.

Neither does this mean that Christianity is unconcerned with law or property. Things must be done decently and in order, if people are to have freedom and time for the ultimate pursuits that add to the dignity of human life. It enriches life to own property. But the main point is that society must never think of its members as mere taxpayers, or customers, or consumers, who exist to make a system operate. It is entirely the other way around, and our message is that tyranny and exploitation cannot last in a universe which has set persons at the center as the chief value.

Nearly a hundred years ago, John Stuart Mill in his famous essay on liberty spoke the truth which we cannot consider too often:

> The state which dwarfs its men, in order that they may be more docile instruments in its hands even for beneficial purposes, will find that with small men no great thing can be accomplished; and that the perfection of machinery to which it has sacrificed everything, will in the end avail it nothing, for want

of the vital power which in order that the machine might work more smoothly, it has preferred to banish.[2]

This is the good news which the Christian prophet always proclaims. If it is judgment to the exploiter and tyrant, it is refreshment to every man yearning to breathe free.

2. JOY

These things I have spoken to you, that my joy may be in you, and that your joy may be full. JOHN 15:11

It will come as a shock to many people that Christianity is supposed to be full of joy. Any number of young people have raised their eyebrows in surprise when I have announced to them that it is a lot of fun to be a Christian. This means that because of some strange misunderstanding of their Lord, too many of his disciples feel they do him the best service if their hearts are heavy and their mood is black. There has grown up in our thinking, therefore, the false impression that paganism is a kind of spontaneous happiness, while Christianity is dour and grim. It is rather distressing to note the number of laymen as well as preachers who can discourse interestingly and spontaneously on every subject except religion. Once that subject is announced, a kind of pall seems to settle down over the assembly.

I met a chaplain when on a preaching mission for the Air Force in Europe, who said that he had discovered people were much more ready to talk about religion after having a few drinks. This chaplain, obviously not a Methodist, then inquired if I had not discovered the same thing to be true. The truth is I had not, for a Methodist bishop receives very few invitations which make it possible to observe this phe-

[2] *Mill on Liberty,* The Harvard Classics, vol. 25, Collier & Son, 1909, 325.

nomenon at close range. But I have been thinking about what he said. His explanation was that people are so tied up inside, so tense and fearful, that it takes alcohol to relax them sufficiently to discuss profound spiritual matters. He insisted that some of his best pastoral work has been done at cocktail parties. He did confess, however, that he had made no survey to determine what, if any, lasting results such pastoral work accomplished.

If what that chaplain said was true—and I have no reason to doubt him—is there perhaps another explanation possible? Has Christianity become so heavy and so prosaic that men cannot bear to discuss it naturally unless they have had their repressions put to sleep temporarily? Has religion become so unnatural and stuffy that men stay away from it as if it were the plague? What has happened to the element of joy which is so obvious in the Gospels?

Now the most amazing thing about the joy expressed in the New Testament is that it was not dependent upon escape from trouble. Quite the opposite! It was joy which men found in the midst of adversity and untoward circumstances. We look back upon those people and marvel that they had so little which we believe necessary for happiness. There were so many things in their lives to spell defeat and failure. The author of Hebrews, for example, can urge Christians to remember that they are surrounded by witnesses; that they should run with their eyes "looking to Jesus the pioneer and perfector of our faith, who for the joy that was set before him endured the cross, despising the shame, and is seated at the right hand of the throne of God" (Hebrews 12:2). We must not lose sight of that marvelous insight, that our Lord, even when moving toward crucifixion and death, had joy set before him and lived by it.

Or if we turn to the Apostle Paul, we wonder mightily at what he had found in his life to cause rejoicing. Here is the record:

> Five times I have received at the hands of the Jews the forty lashes less one. Three times I have been beaten with rods; once I was stoned. Three times I have been shipwrecked; a night and a day I have been adrift at sea; on frequent journeys, in danger from rivers, danger from robbers, danger from my own people, danger from Gentiles, danger in the city, danger in the wilderness, danger at sea, danger from false brethren; in toil and hardship, through many a sleepless night, in hunger and thirst, often without food, in cold and exposure. And, apart from other things, there is the daily pressure upon me of my anxiety for all the churches. II CORINTHIANS 11:24–28

Yet this is the man who can hardly write concerning the greatest difficulties and biggest disappointments without breaking forth with a command to rejoice. One of the underlying themes running through all of Paul's letters is summed up in his word to the Philippians: "Rejoice in the Lord always; again I will say, Rejoice" (Philippians 4:4). Whatever the source of the joy may have been, it certainly was not escape from heavy burdens and grievous sufferings.

What has been said about Jesus and Paul could be said to some extent at least about those early Christians. There was certainly no social advantage in becoming a part of the Christian fellowship, and common sense must have told them that they took great risks. If there was to be a victory in the future, it was not observable in the first or second centuries. Yet these people, who seemed to be always in trouble and were regarded as troublemakers turning things upside down, had a spontaneous happiness bubbling up within them that was one of the main sources of their power. If they were right, then we have been wrong. For our assumption has been that joy depends upon outward circumstance and physical comfort. They found it in something which denied the final reality of adversity or persecution. That the New Testament should be a book of seriousness and have within it a pending sense of tragedy should not surprise us in the least. But that the New Testament at the same time is a joyful book, telling about an experience of blessedness in the midst of pain, is one of the miracles of the Bible which has been overlooked.

No matter what the early Christians faced, they had the sense of an ultimate victory. There was something about the Christian experience which gave an assurance of triumph, and this created joy. It is meaninglessness and uncertainty that robs life of its happiness. But the man who knows that the enterprise he has given his life to is destined to overcome the world will find satisfaction even in the midst of adversity.

We do not make enough of the gaiety of Christians. We do not make enough of the sheer pleasure which comes to preachers. It is my belief that no profession in the world brings so much satisfaction to its members as the Christian ministry. One encounters more humor and joy of living among preachers than among any other group. Yet they do not give this impression to the laity very often. George Wharton Pepper, the lawyer layman who gave the Beecher Lectures in 1915, comments on this tendency to become grim-faced and sanctimonious in proclaiming the gospel. He writes:

> Sometime ago I was one of a great audience assembled to hear Mr. Sunday. Among all those present were college students. Before he began to speak, the young faces had upon them a curious

and unnatural look of depression. "Cheer up!" said the evangelist, "you're not in church." The effect was electric. The students became boys again. The speaker, by a single stroke, had broken down their reserve. I do not stop to argue the question whether the evangelist ought to have said it, or whether his implication was or was not fair to the clergy. I merely record the fact that several thousand young men, whether justly or unjustly, were obviously accustomed to associate preaching with gloom.[3]

There is no greater engine for the production of moral power than joy. What man among us could be of heavy heart, and dour countenance, if he really believed that there walks beside him one who says, "I have said this to you, that in me you may have peace. In the world you have tribulation; but be of good cheer, I have overcome the world" (John 16:33). Men who truly believe in their cause and its final triumph move into the battle with a song in their hearts and a smile on their faces. It was to men who had this experience fresh in their lives that St. Paul addressed his letters. From hatred and sadness they entered into delight and love, so that to restore their spiritual health the Apostle can simply remind them of the difference between the world and the Kingdom of God. He writes:

> Now the works of the flesh are plain: immorality, impurity, licentiousness, idolatry, sorcery, enmity, strife, jealousy, anger, selfishness, dissension, party spirit, envy, drunkenness, carousing, and the like. . . . But the fruit of the Spirit is love, joy, peace, patience, kindness, goodness, faithfulness, gentleness, self-control; against such there is no law. GALATIANS 5:19–23

Perhaps in no other way do we so clearly bear testimony of our loss of Christian faith as in our failure to associate

[3] Jones, *The Royalty of the Pulpit,* Harper, 1951, 357.

companionship with Jesus Christ with the emotion of joy. Saved from despair, doubt and fear, Christians are redeemed by their happy faith.

This means that the preacher or the layman who professes to know Christ and has no laughter is deceiving himself. The kind of narrow, mean, intolerant bitterness which sometimes passes for orthodoxy may be a kind of religion, but it is not Christian. There are few things which would so restore the church to its true nature and put Christianity on the offensive again as preachers showing by their words and their lives that they have been taken hold of by joy unspeakable and full of glory.

Charles W. Elliott attended church in London, then wrote home to his son Samuel giving his commentary on the experience:

> Yesterday we attended M's church and heard an excellent sermon badly delivered. The whole service lacked cheerfulness. The tones of M's voice and his inflections were all depressing! It is almost the worst of faults in a preacher. Faith, hope and love are all cheerful things and ought to be made to appear so by those who preach them. Life is not always bright, but religion should be.[4]

If we have no answer, then we ought not to preach. But if we have an answer to man's need and to the world's condition, that answer should be described in cheerful tones. The French poet, Claudel, once said that after he had heard Beethoven's Fifth Symphony he knew that at the heart of the universe there is joy. How much more then should those who have been found by God in Christ be certain that whatever else they have been commanded to speak, they must

[4] Ralph Ward, Jr., *Zions Herald,* Dec. 3, 1952.

certainly speak gladness. We who preach ought to read the Christmas story in Luke every Sunday before we enter our pulpits and remember that we too proclaim "good news of a great joy which will come to all the people."

3. FREEDOM

Is not this the fast that I choose: to loose the bonds of wickedness, to undo the thongs of the yoke, to let the oppressed go free, and to break every yoke? ISAIAH 58:6

One of the most disturbing and shocking things about our generation has been its willingness to give up freedom in so many places in the world. When Mussolini said in the early days of his rise to power that men had, perhaps, grown weary of liberty, we did not take him seriously. But the events which followed proved him to be right, and in nation after nation men allowed their liberties to slip away from them without showing very much concern. This is possible, of course, only when men assume that freedom is an option. Back of the whole debacle there is the philosophy which regards liberty as perhaps nice to have under some circumstances but not as a necessity. It is assumed that while some people are willing to fight for freedom, others are quite willing to live without it, and in either case, it is a matter of personal taste.

Fortunately for this generation we have seen a number of experiments tried in the realm of totalitarianism. We ought to know now that freedom instead of being an option is an absolute necessity for a healthy society. The totalitarian regimes all begin bravely, but they all end badly. If we look at the record, we shall be convinced that God made men for freedom and there is no good news that does not proclaim it.

We should not forget how the original advantage seemed

to be all with the Nazis. There was a time when only men of great faith believed that this evil could be turned back. Yet when free men finally rallied together, the tide was turned and the Nazis were battered into unconditional surrender. The one thing which should not be overlooked is that the scientific research necessary for survival found its chance among free men and not among slaves. I have seen enough evidence to convince me that one of the reasons the Nazis lost the war was their creation of an atmosphere of fear and their narrow dogmatism which made research limp timidly when it should have run freely. If a nation expects to survive, it had better provide freedom for its scientists if for no higher motive than self-preservation.

We know enough about the Communist regime in Russia to see that it has destroyed art. The novelist who has to make sure that what he says will please the Kremlin cannot set his imagination free to create a living book. If a poet must write "communistic poetry" it becomes no more than propaganda. The musician who has to find out, if he can, what kind of music will please the party leaders will never be able to create music for the ages. If an artist has to be sure that his work will fit the demands of a totalitarian government, his inspiration dies before it can find wings. If man is to create, then man must be free.

Let America understand this truth now and always. Let us all understand that we are dealing here with a necessity, because man is made in the image of God. The champion of freedom becomes more than just an individual, for he represents the hope of mankind. The Christian preacher in this and every generation finds the authority for his message of freedom in the very nature of things, which is to say, in God.

If it is true that the foundation of a democracy is free public education, then it must follow that whatever threatens our schools is a threat to our country. We must believe in the ability and the willingness of men to choose the truth, once they can see what the truth is. If we threaten our teachers with investigations aimed at attacking all unorthodox opinions, then only second-rate men will go into the teaching profession. For safety's sake they will deal with dead issues and not live ones, and by this madness practically assure the deterioration of our national life. If we make men afraid to join any organization lest it be discovered that a subversive fellow once was a member of it, then we drive men into isolated fear instead of in the direction of cooperative faith. America has been a nation of joiners from the beginning. Part of the strength of our people has been that men of like mind have met together and organized societies for the promulgation of their interests and ideas. This began at least as early as Benjamin Franklin.

As wise an observer as Alex de Toqueville observed that the greatness of America was in its free pulpits preaching righteousness. No man truly proclaims the good news unless he proclaims freedom and if by any chance the preacher joins too many of his brethren in keeping silent when he should speak, then he has betrayed his commission and mutilated his word. Men must be free, not because it is a nice thing, but because it is an essential thing. Men can never enter into their heritage unless they are free, and that freedom, of course, begins in a man's conquest of sin and self. The Gospel proclaiming that in Christ men can master themselves defines the foundation of a free society.

It is my conviction that we have not made enough of the unity of freedom. Is it merely a coincidence that Protestantism with its emphasis on the priesthood of all believers is the mother of democracy and free enterprise? I think not. The man who is not free religiously cannot be free politically or economically. For underneath our whole social structure there is the spirit of the individual whose freedom, or lack of it, colors and sharpens society. When a man's consciousness of his glorious status as God's free creature grows dim, then the light begins to go out in all his relationships.

When a Jewish officer in the French Army had been successfully forced into a scapegoat role by a reactionary military regime, it must have seemed that the case would not come up again. For a ruling was handed down by the court that the issue could never be raised, since it had already been adjudicated. But Emile Zola insisted on probing into the Dreyfus affair again, and he was brought to trial. As Zola's lawyer came to the end of his great defense, he pointed to the crucifix which hung over the judge's seat. Raising his voice, he said, "They called that case closed too." So it is that the reactionary forces from time to time try to close the case on man's freedom and wipe from every constitution his right to question tyranny. But even as the One who was crucified could not be dealt with in such a fashion, neither can the freedom which men have found in him be denied. Ours is the good news that because we are the sons of God we are born into liberty. Our word is the command of our God "to let the oppressed go free."

4. POWER

Behold, I have given you authority to tread upon serpents and scorpions, and over all the power of the enemy; and nothing shall hurt you. LUKE 10:19

Let us not forget that the promise of the Gospel is not

ease, but power. Our first impulse when things are difficult is to pray that something will make them easier for us. If a load is heavy, we cry out that the load be made lighter. If the obstacle is before us, we pray that it may be removed. If this does not happen—and usually it does not—then we listen to the seductive voice promising the secret of how to get along with the difficulty without too much pain or tension. We call it adjustment.

The popular psychological idea of our time is that we should learn to live within our environment without strain. This almost always leads us in the direction of adjusting our tasks to our strength and finding a way to live easily with our problems. Yet if adjustment to the environment is the ultimate goal of life, we should expect very little spiritual or intellectual growth. I remember seeing some hogs wallowing in a mudhole on a Nebraska farm, and that picture always comes back to me when I think of adjustment. They were perfectly adjusted; never raising a question about cleaning up the mudhole nor striving to live on a higher level. We should be reminded also that during the war this philosophy was accepted by a number of people in the occupied countries. They said that since the enemy was there they might as well trade with him, co-operate with him, and make a profit if possible. The whole idea was adjustment and it seemed to work very well. The only thing wrong was that after the enemy had been driven out, these men who had been so wise as to adjust were called collaborators. Some of them were hanged. For men seem to have the rather strange idea that there are many times when you have no right to adjust, but must resist.

There is some contemporary preaching which has quite missed the way because it has been infiltrated by a psychological lust for ease, and it describes feverishly a life without tension. In every large city you can discover a number of pulpits advertising sermons on how to stop worrying or how to make life easier. It is amazing to note the number of churches that have allowed themselves to become nothing more than centers of distribution for religious aspirin tablets and mental opiates. Such preaching is not Christian and fundamentally it is not even good advice. A preacher who believes that all that men want is release from their difficulties is a man who does not know mankind very well.

Consider Jeremiah, in so many ways a man with few peers in religion. When it comes to spiritual insight and moral courage, there are not many to sit beside him. But by no stretch of the imagination can he be called an integrated personality. According to his autobiography, which runs through his preaching, he seldom if ever knew peace. He was desperately in need of a visit from a minister skilled in pastoral psychology. But more important than integration, Jeremiah found power to answer God's summons to do his duty and accept his destiny. It did not give him either mental or spiritual relaxation, but it made him one of the greatest interpreters of God's will who ever lived.

What men are actually seeking is an adequacy like Jeremiah's. If I know my own heart at all, I know that rather than have the burden taken from me, I would prefer to be strong enough to bear the burden. Rather than have the responsibility placed on somebody else's shoulders, I would prefer the ability to see the job through to the end. For the first crying out of pain is not the real truth about us, but merely the natural reaction against the immediate discomfort. The man who can live with himself with any kind of satisfaction has to believe that he is strong enough to bear real burdens and has character enough to do his duty. St. Paul speaks for all mankind when he tells about his thorn in the flesh:

> Three times I besought the Lord about this, that it should leave me; but he said to me, "My grace is sufficient for you, for my power is made perfect in weakness." I will all the more gladly boast of my weaknesses, that the power of Christ may rest upon me. II CORINTHIANS 12:8–9

The promise of the Gospel is not ease.

When my brother-in-law returned from the war, he wanted to build a home but found the cost prohibitive. He decided to build it himself, acting as his own contractor and doing much of the actual work himself. Every free moment for almost a year was spent in the building, and finally it was finished. I can remember one night visiting with some friends in his home, and talking after dinner about the completion of the hard job. A mutual friend said, "Jim, I did not think you could ever do it, but you did." I glanced at my brother-in-law, who is a very modest person, and saw a quiet look of satisfaction on his face which comes to a man who has seen a long and exhausting project through to the end. I thought to myself then that here is what men really want, and without it they are never quite satisfied. The good news of the Gospel is that men may have power.

Some time ago a mine shaft collapsed. Immediately a rescue crew was organized to dig to the trapped men before their air was exhausted. As they approached the doomed miners, they thought they heard a tapping on the rocks and paused to listen. In Morse code there came the question, "Is there any hope? Is there any hope?" Ours is the good news to every man trapped by his own weakness and his own fear, that there is hope. To men caught in frustration, failure, and despair the Gospel is the good news of power enough to live nobly and heroically.

5. FOR THE PREACHER

. . . set apart for the gospel of God. . . . ROMANS 1:1

There are different, discouraging things about the ministry, especially if he does not achieve what we call success. My heart goes out to that man who started so bravely but finally has to confess to himself that some of his friends have passed him by and he is not destined for the big pulpit and the large congregation. Then he is in danger lest he grow bitter, or what is in some ways worse, grow dull. Having lost the encouragement of advancement, he may lose the sense of the dignity of his calling and the crucial nature of his word.

Yet this is not inevitable, for some of the most dynamic personalities I ever met have been ministers of smaller churches. With a wonderful debonair quality in their speaking and living, they have influenced men and brought a golden glow to many a fading enthusiasm. As I have tried to analyze this quality, it seems to me that it rests in a very high view of their commission. They never take lightly their preaching function and they have a profound faith in the power of their "good news."

But even the man who gets on in the church will not be proof against the temptation to play down the majestic uniqueness of the Gospel. Such a man may face those terrible moments when he knows that Christianity has become to him a mere means to a living, but no longer the power of God to every man who hears him. He becomes a good performer in a profession that has its share of poor ones, and the people who direct the life of his congregation will congratulate themselves on having a man who is "ready and able to improvise entertainingly on the sublimest Christian ministry as well as on the most touchy, the most delicate and scabrous of parochial issues."[5] Such men have their reward, but it is not enough.

This whole business is aggravated by the lack of enthusiasm and zeal in the average congregation. A minister does not arrive in a church, as a rule, that is breathlessly awaiting his command to march. He has to overcome lethargy and awaken the drowsy. The soft-spoken objective man may be a very fine person in all ways, but the church needs a man whose faith blazes from his eyes and vibrates through the tones of his voice. Let him say every time he enters his pulpit, "I have good news for these people." We would do well to remember that so much of the emphasis of Paul and John was on the gift of eternal life. It could be said of them and of every great evangelist what the serving maid in Stephen Vincent Benét's *A Child Is Born* says of the shepherds: "They were drunk with the good news." So were Peter and his companions on the Day of Pentecost. It is a fine, legitimate intoxication for the preacher.

On March 29, 1739, John Wesley wrote in his *Journal:*

> Sat. 31st.—In the evening I reached Bristol, and met Mr. Whitefield there. I could scarcely reconcile myself at first to this strange way of preaching in the fields, of which he set me an example on Sunday; having been all my life (till very lately) so tenacious of every point relating to decency and order, that I should have thought the saving of souls almost a sin, if it had not been done in a church.

[5] Huxley, *The Devils of Loudon,* Harper, 1952, 19.

It is of more than merely historical interest that like Another preaching in the synagogue of Nazareth he chose as his text on that momentous occasion:

> The Spirit of the Lord is upon me, because he has anointed me to preach good news to the poor. He has sent me to proclaim release to the captives and recovery of sight to the blind, to set at liberty those who are oppressed, to proclaim the acceptable year of the Lord. LUKE 4:18

The power of the Evangelical Revival was in its faith and affirmation, that whatever men had done and whatever their condition might be, there was a good word for them to hear. To every human problem Wesley and his followers believed there was a solution in the Gospel.

Ghost writing has been a profession, and at least one college offers a course in it. While business executives are prone to have their speeches prepared in this manner, one of them finally rebelled. The head of Olin Industries arose to read a ghost-written speech, and after five minutes stopped and tore it up. "Gentlemen," he said, "don't believe a word I have said! Now here is what I really want to say." There are preachers whose discourses sound impersonal, borrowed, and only half-absorbed. Tear them up, brethren, and speak what you know and believe about the good news. Ten words of experience are worth ten thousand words of theory.

Now if this is our viewpoint, then it will certainly cure us of pulpit tones, consciously refined pronunciations, and all those little tricks which brand us as fakes. My heart goes out to that strange young man Salinger wrote about in *The Catcher in the Rye,* and especially when he says:

> If you want to know the truth, I can't even stand ministers. The ones they've had at every school I've gone to, they all have

these Holy Joe voices when they start giving their sermons. . . .
They sound so phony when they talk.[6]

But what man can talk like that if he is bursting with an announcement that spells the difference between heaven and hell for every man who hears him?

This whole concept of the Christian message as good news demands a delivery free from manuscript and notes. That statement will start an argument in any preachers' meeting, but I have yet to meet a layman who disagrees with it. The men who sit in the pews are agreed that, other things being equal, they will choose the man who can speak without notes every time. They have a true feeling that real preaching is direct, simple, and without written barriers. In fact, they go further than homiletical professors think proper. But they are right, and we will do well to trust their judgment. When John Wesley preached his famous sermon "On the Death of the Rev. Mr. George Whitefield" on November 18, 1770, he remarked that "it was on the 29th [of December] that he first preached without notes." Wesley rightly assumed that such an occasion should never be forgotten. My brethren, it is a crucial and glorious day in any man's ministry when he decides to stand on his feet without any other support save preparation and the Holy Spirit, and preach.

There are enough men who maintain the sparkle of the New Testament to show that it can be done. Mark Twain, for example, had a real fondness for clergymen. He called on them in little western towns and for the most part found them to be delightful companions. Mark had a real respect for the ministry and when he was a boy, he considered

[6] Salinger, *The Catcher in the Rye,* Little, Brown, 1945.

entering the ministry himself because, as he said, "it never occurred to me that a preacher could be damned." A friend of his did enter the ministry and became a country preacher with barely enough income to keep him alive. After twenty years Mark wrote to him: "I am glad you are in the ministry. It is the highest dignity to which a man may aspire."[7] I suggest that a profession which could gain the respect of a man like Mark Twain ought not to be stuffy or pompous. "If heresy has slain its thousands, then monotony has slain its tens of thousands."[8] We must confess that some of us will have to fight harder than others against this enemy of all public speakers. Some men cannot be dull if they try, and others, unfortunately, can be terribly dull without half trying. But if the full import of what God has proclaimed to us through Christ once strikes us, our words will come alive and march into the hearts of our hearers. Let us not oversimplify a very serious problem, but let us attack the problem at the root. We must realize afresh that, compared with the excitement, and the awful significance of our word, the most lurid headlines of the morning newspaper partake of the nature of obituary notices.

A word of warning needs to be spoken. We have had men in modern pulpits who understood the need of being interesting, but they conceived it too narrowly. An after-dinner speaker is one thing and a preacher is another. To be just entertaining is well enough for a lecture, though even then it is very difficult without some serious theme running through it. But let such a brother try it week after week before the same people, then it becomes apparent that frothy humor and shallow cleverness are the most boring things

[7] Wecter, *Sam Clemens of Hannibal,* Houghton Mifflin, 1952, 231.

[8] James, *William Russell Maltby, Obiter Scripta,* Epworth, 1952, 99.

in the world. People will come a few times and then stay away in crowds. There can be no continuous ministry without the imagination to see excitement in Christian doctrine, and enough historical knowledge to make the creeds live. There is no other theme upon which a man may discourse week after week without monotony but the Gospel of Jesus Christ. Do not make the mistake of skimming the surface, but go down deep, brethren, deep down.

One of the great hymns loved and sung by Americans is "America the Beautiful." The words are by Katharine Lee Bates and the music was composed by Samuel A. Ward. But a man whose name does not appear in connection with the hymn was a Baptist preacher of Rochester who brought the words and the music together. It is not too much to say that his was also a creative act. Which is a parable! When a preacher brings the Gospel and a man together, the result is "a new creature," and although he did not write the good news nor make the man's heart respond, still his was the role of the creator too. And it is the highest dignity which is ever bestowed on a man, for in the words of Paul, it is nothing less than being "set apart to declare God's good news" (Romans 1:1, Goodspeed).

II *Good News of Action*

> And Jesus said to them "Follow me and I will make you become fishers of men." And immediately they left their nets and followed him. MARK 1:17

The earliest and shortest of the Gospels gives us a portrait of one who was the incarnation of God's action. Here is a life story which is theology in deeds and doctrine in drama. Mark is most impressed with the things which Jesus does and his book is a recitation of the mighty works of God in Christ. All philosophical and intellectual considerations are very much in the background and the teachings of Jesus are short, sharp utterances of insight and command. That which was previously cloudy or vague has become concrete in a life. The significance of Jesus for Mark is his personal, active relationship to God and to other persons. He is no other-worldly saint who withdraws from men to contemplate God, but an action which breaks into human experience with something unique and overpowering. Mark would have no difficulty in accepting the modern existentialist insistence that the only reality is action.

This underlying conception of the nature of the good

news affects the style and the vocabulary of Mark. He has the gift of eliminating the unnecessary detail so that the dramatic impact may be even more powerful. Consider the unforgettable effect of such a sentence as this: "And they crucified him, and divided his garments among them, casting lots for them, to decide what each should take." (15:24) If we assume, as do most modern scholars, that the original Mark ended with the words "for they were afraid" (16:8), we do not wonder that the early church preferred a Gospel with more detail. His brevity is amazing as we consider that he has no story of Jesus' birth, no Sermon on the Mount, and comparatively few parables. He moves as fast as he possibly can and yet the seeds of all the fundamental Christian affirmations are found in this shortest of the Gospels.[1]

This matter of vocabulary should not be missed by preachers. Charles Kingsley, it may be remembered, portrays the wife of the country squire of Harthover House as making certain vocabulary suggestions which William Jewett Tucker passed along to Yale student ministers a long time ago.

> So she made Sir John write to the "Times" to command the Chancellor of the Exchequer for the time being to put a tax on long words: a light tax on words over three syllables, which are necessary evils, like rats, but which like them must be kept down judiciously; a heavy tax on words of over four syllables, such as heterodoxy, spontaneity, spuriosity, and the like, and on words of over five syllables a totally prohibitory tax, and a similar prohibitory tax on words derived from three or four languages at the same time.[2]

If Mark were written in our modern times we might say

[1] See Rieu, *Introduction to the Four Gospels,* Penguin, 1953.
[2] Jones, *op. cit.,* 190.

of it, as of some contemporary novels, that the author seems to have his eye on Hollywood and is writing an elaborated scenario. This could hardly be called a treatise or even a biography. Actually it is a series of sharp events held together with rather tenuous connections which serve to carry us forward to the ultimate and final action, namely, the Crucifixion and Resurrection.

The Sunday School boy grasped a central idea when he heard his teacher read the early paragraphs of Mark. He said, "He sure got round over the ground fast." [3]

One of the legitimate reasons for using the new translations is to get into the atmosphere of the stark urgency of Mark. We do not get it in the King James Version and most of our reading of the English Bible has given us a false idea of a book that is never leisurely or philosophical in the original, but tends to take on this tone when we read it in Elizabethan English. Too many modern Christians think that Mark is chamber music, while in reality he is a trumpet.

In one of his books, the late Willard L. Sperry, one-time dean of Harvard Divinity School, relates that two classical Greek scholars were speaking together and one asked the other if he had read the New Testament recently. The man confessed that he had not, but agreed to read the Gospel of Mark. Some time later they met again and the classical scholar was asked what impression Mark had made on him. He said he was impressed most of all with its violence. Not many people in the congregation have that impression when they hear the Gospel of Mark read from the pulpit nor do they get that idea when they hear a preacher speak of the message which springs out of it. It may be well for us to

[3] Love, *The Gospel and the Gospels,* Abingdon, 1953, 145.

consider anew that our message according to Mark is the good news of action.

1. GOD

He is not God of the dead, but of the living. . . . MARK 12:27

The God of the Bible is the Creator whose presence is made known by what He has done in nature, in history, and by what He is demanding of His children presently. When the Book of Genesis begins with its mighty affirmation that "in the beginning God created the heavens and the earth," it is saying an essential thing about the nature of God. While there have been some foolish people through the years who have hoped to confine God's activity to some special day or occasion, He breaks forth continually in human experience with an unmistakable sign of His continuing creative activity. He seems to have something on His mind and now and again a prophet has arisen with a vision of that far-off divine event toward which God directs men and their world. Any philosophy therefore which speaks of an "unmoved mover" is contrary to our religion. The Christian philosopher must always understand reality in terms of process, even as A. N. Whitehead has so clearly pointed out. William James had the truth of it when he wrote:

> The prince of darkness may be a gentleman, as we are told he is, but whatever the God of earth and heaven is, he can surely be no gentleman. His menial services are needed in the depths of our human trials, even more than his dignity is needed in the empyrean.[4]

I have never been able to understand why modern Christians have been upset by modern science. It would seem ap-

[4] James, *Pragmatism*, 72.

parent that if God is as the Bible describes Him, then the world must be as modern science describes it. It is a world of energy in which the old concepts of matter and static masses no longer avail. Things flow, move, react, and instead of reducing everything to materiality, the universe must be seen in terms of energy. The atom, which has within it such explosive powers for good or ill, is a revelation indeed of the God whose creation contains terrifying, marvelous activity. Harry Emerson Fosdick relates that he looked up a dictionary definition of uranium a few years back, and read: "Uranium is a rare, heavy, greyish, metallic element, with no important uses." It is a wonderful, though sometimes frightening, experience to contemplate a world which underneath even its drabbest appearance is dynamite and lightning. Science adds its voice to Mark's and proclaims that our God has created a world of such inexhaustible energy that action must be an essential part of His nature.

But the scandal of all this is that the same God who creates is involved in the struggles of His creation. The Bible has a proper understanding of the wonder of the heavens and the glory of the world. But it is not so impressed with nature's majesty as with the God who heals the broken heart and lifts up the fallen. Why should he get mixed up in all this mess? That is now and always has been the question of the intelligentsia and the philosophical. It is the marvel of the religious man and he has no clear answer to it except he knows that somehow the human struggle is of utter importance to God, because He has thrown himself into it and He has committed Himself to its victorious solution. Not in a cold, merciless justice do we see Him, therefore, but in a suffering love which takes unto itself the disasters and the defeats of men.

We have no hesitancy in telling others to "mind their own business" whenever their activities interfere with our convenience. No one experiences this more often than the preacher, except God. We tell Him continuously that we are happy for His interests here but not there. We are willing for Him to act on other people and call other nations to account, but not us. Yet His business seems to be with all of creation, especially men. In our pride and arrogancy we accuse Him of meddling, though in our best moments we are made humble and thankful by His concern. But however we may take it, one thing is certain. God's business is with each man, at all times, under every condition.

A few years ago I was giving some lectures at Union Theological Seminary in New York City. In between my own lectures I sat at the feet of a great teacher, and one morning he used a phrase that shocked me profoundly. I am not too easily shocked, but these words seemed lacking in a proper respect for Deity. The lecturer said that there is a sense in which God is to be thought of as the celestial garbage collector. He then went on to point out that life without God becomes intolerable because the poisons and wastes of sin pile up until men find themselves living on a garbage heap with the stench of it in their nostrils. Some power has to keep life sanitary and livable. That is what God does. He sterilizes the impure so that men may have an atmosphere clean enough for healthy living. He is the God of redeeming action indeed but not action from a distance.

In the last century the president of an American theological seminary, coming to the close of a long administration, boasted that under his leadership no new idea had ever been put forth in the school. He meant to imply, no doubt, that he had been orthodox in the beginning and had never changed. All he was doing, however, was confessing to a stale, petrified theology that could not interpret a living God. The God of the living has more light to break forth on us than we shall ever be able to receive. But if the message of Mark has reached its goal, we shall have great expectations that perhaps around the next corner we shall see Him anew and He will reveal to us an activity which shall take us into a deeper awareness of His presence.

2. MAN

. . . but whoever would be great among you must be your servant, and whoever would be first among you must be slave of all. MARK 10:43–44

A social system can be judged by the number of men it condemns to be bystanders. The way of life that sentences thousands of people to look on while others participate in the affairs of society and make the decisions is certainly a denial of the Christian understanding of the nature of man. Henry T. Hodgkin said, "Every great religious awakening has been a revolt against authority." But I think it is even better to say that every religious awakening has been a revolt against neglect. Men get tired of being regarded as unimportant. When the Gospel calls them to an activity which is deemed significant, they claim their heritage, and the new revival is born.

Certainly that was true of the early Christians. St. Paul writes:

For consider your call, brethren; not many of you were wise according to worldly standards, not many were powerful, not

many were of noble birth; but God chose what is foolish in the world to shame the wise, God chose what is weak in the world to shame the strong, God chose what is low and despised in the world, even things that are not, to bring to nothing things that are, so that no human being might boast in the presence of God.
I CORINTHIANS 1:26–29

The Christian faith was as a trumpet call to men proclaiming that there is a foe; there is a faith; and there is a victory. There was nothing in the nature of an opiate about it, and instead of protecting men, it threw them into the arena. But the important thing to remember is that most of those who responded had never been regarded as important enough to enlist in a significant enterprise. Yet they were the ones who constituted not only the private soldiers but the officers of the new army.

The early Methodists illustrate the same truth. I have been astounded in recent times to discover the widely held contemporary opinion of the early followers of John Wesley. The respectable churchgoing people not only despised them for their lack of social graces, but they feared them as ignorant, enthusiastic subversives. But many a man found for the first time when a Methodist Class Meeting gave him his chance, that he could organize a group and lead it. Many a man found he could speak with power, by learning to stand on his feet and witness to his new experience. Or to put it in another way, like the early Christians, the early Methodists were saved by the good news of action.

Our modern tendency is to sentimentalize and soften the very concept of the spiritual. We offer it to tired, troubled people as if it were escape from the battle. To become spiritual seems to mean we can call it a day. We make it something delicate and tender. It is like taking a hot bath to get relaxed and ready for sleep. But the Bible regards the Spirit of God as anything but a soporific, and the man who has been clothed with God's Spirit goes forth to do mighty works and perform heroic tasks. It was this spiritual power that Jesus promised his followers and they knew that this was the essential thing they lacked.

One of the leaders of the Norwegian underground during the Nazi occupation was describing some of his experiences during that harrowing period. He told about the narrow escapes, the constant danger, the threat of torture, and the exhausting tasks. And then he said in a kind of wonderment that one day it came to him he was what men would call a happy man. Perhaps the "peace of mind" school had better ponder the implications of such a testimony.

A man married a woman belonging to one of the new sects which stresses the conquest of evil by thinking the right thoughts. He had no religion of his own, so he joined and tried earnestly to be a faithful member of the group. After some time had passed, he resigned, and when one of his friends asked him the reason, he replied, "I got tired of being so blank happy." It is not the struggle that destroys us, but the sense of not being there when the real battle is being fought. Albert Edward Day tells of a lifeboat at sea. One big fellow, frightened by the danger, said that he was going to stop rowing and pray. But a hard-boiled sailor snapped out, "Let the little fellow pray, you stick to the oars."[5] We do not mean to imply that prayer and meditation are to be discarded, but we do mean to insist that men are meant to act, and the Gospel is a pronouncement of doom on any way of life that denies this heritage to every person.

In the story of the cursing of the fig tree, Mark adds the

[5] Day, *An Autobiography of Prayer,* Harper, 1952, 137.

words: "it was not the season for figs" (11:13). This has caused a great deal of debate because it sounds like an irritated, petulant, unreasonable attitude on the part of Jesus. It does not seem to fit his character. But if we consider that Oriental fig trees bear their fruit before their leaves, then this particular tree had freakishly put forth its leaves out of season and so appeared to be ahead of time with its fruit. But this was all misleading appearance without reality. Perhaps we have here an indication of Jesus' hatred of hypocrisy and pretense. Men are supposed to deliver what they claim to possess, and they must be judged by their fruits and not the attractiveness of their leaves.

Possessions never prove to be an adequate substitute for meaningful activity. Remember the words of the rich young man who came to Jesus saying, "Good teacher, what must I do to inherit eternal life?" For him it was no longer a matter of what shall I have or what must I possess. The question for him, as for all men soon or late, is what kind of activity makes life meaningful. Men and women who have come to the age of retirement without anything to fill the empty hours of their days soon either die of sheer boredom or else visit the psychiatrist. Some have looked forward to this experience for many years only to discover that it was a complete denial of the way they want to live. The men who grow old gracefully and victoriously are always those who have significant enterprises which claim their energy to the very last. The happiest old people I meet are those who are still alert to the needs of the community and interested in every activity. They are the ones who spend their freedom in pursuing goals and trying experiments which the obligation of their jobs made impossible.

The aristocratic theories of life assume that a few people

must be regarded as superior while the masses acquiesce. They are not only unchristian but they are unjust and unrealistic. The Gnostic Heresy is with us always, but the Church must see it as a heresy now, as in the beginning. Our good news is that for every man, regardless of his intellectual qualities, there is a job to do and a place to fill. In the divine economy every man is a servant of God and finds his greatness in His service. This divine word destroys the pretensions of a leisure class and establishes the dignity of those who work.

There is a story about two Germans who attended a meeting where the speaker was long and tiresome. Finally, one said to the other, "Let us go." "No," replied the other. "Let's wait for the verb." As Halford Luccock remarked, "The founder of Christianity liked verbs." [6] He liked verbs because he knew that men need to act. Because he knew what was in man, his way of life gives them great verbs to live by, and heroic parts to play.

3. CHRISTIANITY

And he called to him the twelve, and began to send them out two by two, and gave them authority over the unclean spirits. MARK 6:7

Christianity today faces particularly great and formidable rivals. Totalitarianism which is conquered in one place breaks forth somewhere else under a new guise, and its basic conflict with Christian faith concerns the ultimate nature of man. Yet it is an astounding thing that these evil systems of tyranny gain power among men precisely because they offer them what Christianity brought into the world

[6] *Christian Century,* Nov. 12, 1952.

in the beginning, namely, a chance to participate. To the empty men and the hopeless people such a movement as naziism comes offering something to believe, something to join, and something to do.

I remember being in Germany two or three years after Hitler had come to power. I was on a bicycle trip with a friend and one day on the way from Hamburg to Berlin we were joined by a German butcher boy. My German was very inadequate and his English was even worse, but we did manage to communicate after a fashion, and now and again we found an interpreter who could sharpen our general impressions. I discovered this boy was a Nazi and when I tried to find the reason why, it became plain that he was intrigued by the dream of a national future which was to be realized through his efforts as a part of the Nazi movement. Under ordinary circumstances he would be nothing but a butcher boy for as long as he lived, but the Nazis promised him a new nation, a new destiny, and a significant role to play in the achievement of all those promises. It was quite apparent that he knew nothing about Hitler's political program or his philosophy. But he did believe that his own life would achieve a new dignity through his new faith.

We will do well to seek an understanding of what communism offers that so intrigues millions of people throughout the world. How can a materialistic tyranny win the allegiance of the Orient? There may be a clue in a word spoken by a Red soldier to an American soldier in Berlin at the close of the war. He said, "We are happy not because we are rich but because we know where we are going."

Theodore F. Romig in analyzing Communist success says that one of the main factors is its combination of theory with practice. There is for instance a new idea of what a teacher ought to be in China. Into a land that had the Confucianist concept of a scholar as one who is a sedate, withdrawn person memorizing long books, communism came with the idea of a teacher willing to live a courageous and revolutionary life. So in the early days of the Civil War, a high school teacher might be the leader of a guerilla band, and the professor of science might be the brains of a demolition squad. This man believes that it was an appeal to action which attracted a vast number of Chinese people to this movement.[7] More recently a British faculty member of a one-time Christian university in China reported on a sanitary campaign in Peking. Every university professor was asked to catch not fewer than two flies a day, twenty mosquitoes a week, and one rat if possible. This does not in any way whiten the black tyranny of the Chinese Communists. It does suggest that at times the children of darkness are wiser than the children of light.

When Professor M. A. Lineberger came back from the Far East, he said, "The Americans believe in spiritual things but they try to buy them by material means—by dollars, by gifts, by aid. Communists believe in material things but they offer people something to join, something to do, something to fight." Can it be that the Christian faith retreats before enemies making their appeal on a call to action, while the modern church has interpreted its faith as something quiescent, static, and relatively harmless?

And so far as democracy is concerned, this modern crisis will drive us back to a more profound appraisal of its genius, or it will become but a tired philosophy fighting a holding campaign with its back to the wall. The need is for a leadership which can describe for us the dynamic nature of free-

[7] Leber, *World Faith in Action,* Bobbs-Merrill, 1951, 191.

dom. Ours is not a way of life dedicated to reaction, but a faith that men under God can daringly create a better world and a fuller life. Democracy's unlimited dream is so overwhelming that its rivals appear small and fearful in comparison.

Perhaps we have to come back to the truth that the good news of the Gospel is the good news of action. This means that Christianity is not only something one preaches, but it is also something one lives. It is both a proclamation and a demonstration. Nothing makes this more clear than a visit to the mission field. I wish that every Christian preacher would spend enough time visiting Christian missions to see what the Gospel means in a non-Christian society. You will hear no talk there about the individual gospel over against the social gospel. Sometimes the attack is made by battalions on the masses, but more often it is a matter of a single spy telling a man here and there about a better country and the true King. You will find churches where the Gospel is preached every Sabbath, but you will also find schools to show people the kind of education Christianity incorporates. You will see social settlements indicating what the Gospel does in the slum section of a big city. You will observe rural settlement centers to demonstrate what the Gospel does for farmers and their families. Our danger in America is that we shall forget that the majority of the products of our civilization which we value the most are rooted in Christianity and have been tended by Christians. But since the job is not done, neither is the responsibility to be denied that demands the church to be a constant demonstration of what the Christian Gospel produces.

We have done much social work in this nation, and we shall continue to do it. It is important that we should be concerned about the physical conditions of human life. It is a wonderful thing that no person need starve and that we promote community centers where playground facilities are provided for children. But the healing of a man's life demands something more than this, which is the reason why social work divorced from a spiritual interpretation only goes part of the way. It is the good news of the Gospel that men may live in a new environment, have a new citizenship, and indeed may experience a new birth. It is the demonstration of this inner experience that constitutes the healing of the community and ultimately the healing of the nations.

Some time ago I heard six college students report on a journey to the Orient. They came to feel it was necessary for them to visit the students of India and discuss Christianity and democracy with them. They raised their own funds and as one of them said, "When a man in the east gave us fifteen thousand dollars for our journey, even the business administration majors began to believe in God." But in that "Project India" we have the essence of what the Gospel does to men and for men. It sends them forth two by two, or ten by ten, or thousands by thousands. It casts out evil spirits and cleanses men's lives. We ought not to forget that after the Transfiguration, Jesus was met by a man who asked for his healing touch on his sick boy.

The temptation to turn our religion into a legal code is always with us. We get excited about wrong creeds, but we are not disturbed by neutrality and passivism. We are amused when we read a Rabbinical interpretation like the following:

> If, said the law, a person was murdered on the highway and the assassin was not discovered, the nearest town must bring a calf as an atonement. If, however, the corpse was found half way

between two towns, where on the dead body should the measurement begin to determine which town must bring the calf? Rabbi Eliezer said one must measure from the navel, but Rabbi Akiba, with elaborate reasons based on man's creation in the image of God, argued that one must measure from the nose.

Or there is the case of a Russian Mennonite sect which was more concerned with smoking than drinking, because Jesus had said that it is not what goes into a man but what comes out of him which defiles him.

But whenever men lose sight of the central place of faith in action, they will fall into the trap of making secondary things of primary importance. Listen to any self-consciously orthodox Christian talk for five minutes, and he will invariably bewail a failure to put theological propositions into the right form; but he will hardly ever concern himself with how much love is being brought into a situation. One of the most cleansing elements in our religion is the central insistence that in Jesus we have the good news of active service.

The sacraments of the Church are the rehearsals of God's mighty acts in Christ. Baptism is a sign and a seal signifying that a man has become a part of the Church and has entered the Kingdom of God. He has joined something and committed himself through the words spoken and the water applied. God in Christ acts upon the person who takes this step forward. In the observance of Holy Communion, we are made aware once more that our Lord is with us always and, as Henry Sloane Coffin has put it, "He . . . reveals Himself (to employ a New Testament expression) in 'the breaking of bread.' Note the verb of action—'in the breaking.'"[8]

Some time ago Frederick Norwood was telling me some of the stories which have gathered around the famous Joseph

[8] Coffin, *Communion through Preaching,* Scribner, 1952, 6.

Parker, founder of the City Temple, London. He said it was a one-man church and that there was no governing board or committee to take responsibility for the business matters. There was not even a treasurer; the minister paid the bills himself. When they were going to build a new church over on Holburn Viaduct, Dr. Parker went over with an architect, and pointing to a certain place, he said, "Put the pulpit here and build the church around it." But the Church, when it is truly the Church, is never that kind of an organization. It is always a fellowship where each member participates in deciding the issues and making the decisions. Where the Church is the body of Christ, which is its true nature, the more it provides an opportunity for each member to be a part of the Church's action.

John R. Mott's word of more than twenty years ago is still a needed one:

> A multitude of laymen are today in serious danger. It is positively perilous for them to hear more sermons, attend more Bible classes and open forums, and read more religious ethical works, unless accompanying it all there be afforded day by day an adequate outlet for their new-found truth.[9]

The Gospel has not been preached truly when it has been only heard and pondered. The Gospel has been preached and has been truly received when men have been helped to take a step forward in demonstrating what its implication is in their lives.

4. FOR THE PREACHER

. . . lest he come suddenly and find you asleep. MARK 13:36

An old minister one time remarked, "I am not afraid to preach to probationers; I am not afraid to preach to min-

[9] Mott, *Liberating the Lay Forces of Christianity,* Macmillan, 1932, 84.

isters; but there is a thing called a divinity student. God preserve me from it."[10] Most of us will know what the old man meant, but at the same time it should be said that if divinity students are sometimes critical in a discourteous way, they are usually on fire with the idea that the preaching of the Gospel is a call to action. It is too bad when we lose that, and it is the loss of it that waters down the full force of the message. It is easy for the church to fall into what Baker Brownell called "the principle of delayed function." He applied it to the college campus, but it likewise has an application to a congregation. Some within the church assume that we are not to act but merely to listen while the preacher talks about past actions, or perhaps dreams about future actions. The church in our thinking may become something outside of contemporary living. It may seem to have a relevance only for the day that has gone or a day that has not yet been born.

It is a terrible thing for a preacher to lose this compulsion of the Divine Word. Yet it can happen, as the preaching of some of our contemporaries testifies. The man whose chief aim seems to be to rob us of our earnestness by counseling moderation wears away our cutting edge, even as a knife gets dull from too much hacking away at a granite boulder. Then our only safety is in inner fire which sharpens and renews us. Then we may proclaim with Jeremiah:

If I say, "I will not mention him,
  or speak any more in his name,"
there is in my heart as it were a
  burning fire
  shut up in my bones,
And I am weary with holding it in,
  and I cannot.

JEREMIAH 20:9

[10] Jones, *op. cit.*, 147.

Preachers should never forget that we proclaim the drama of decision. We are dealing with truth that makes a difference. Indeed, we have placed into our keeping a point of view which is full of dynamite. The call to repentance is always a demand to turn one's life upside down and set it straight again. Judgment comes not as comfort but as distress. How easy it is for a pulpit to fall into the pit of harmlessness. There are, I am afraid, pulpits which deserve Tallulah Bankhead's devastating description of Hollywood. She writes:

> Timidity was the screen's curse. It still is. In its effort to please everyone, it succeeds in pleasing no one. It's the most frightened industry, art form or opiate ever to solicitate favor. The screen is scared of the churches, of Congress, of the benevolent order of Elks, the American Legion, of the D.A.R., of its own shadow. What it fears beyond all else is ideas. It's devoted to the past, to tried-and-found-wanting, to the museum and the reactionary. When one of its practitioners blurts out the truth, he is looked upon as a mad man.[11]

A static message can be used to bolster up the status quo or comfort the comfortable. But a message of action, full of the terrifying and inspiring ideas of the New Testament will demand that men stop their compromising and make a decision and choose this day whom they will serve.

In the earliest collection of hymns, *For the People Called Methodists,* there is a section entitled "For Believers Fighting." Those are the people to whom we preach and this is the kind of experience we must have in our minds. Life is a struggle and our people are caught in it. Life is not so much objective contemplation as it is existential activity and decision. That preacher who speaks a word which makes people

[11] Bankhead, *Tallulah,* Harper, 1952, 195.

say yes or no has a congregation even when he stabs deep into their hearts with discontent. Pulitzer's aphorism for editorial writers was to spend twenty hours on an editorial and then hold it to twenty lines. It is a good word for men whose speaking demands a decision.

A friend of mine told me of going to church one Sunday and arriving a little early. As she sat there listening to the organ prelude, she overheard a conversation between two men back of her. One was describing the preacher in uncomplimentary tones. He referred to him as being rather egotistical, as being spoiled by the congregation, and as going out of his way to create an issue in the community. The other man said to him, "Then why do you come to hear him every Sunday?" The other man replied, "Because I always have the feeling that he is going to ask a question which sooner or later I will have to answer, and the sooner I answer it the better for me." Let our preaching not be merely the answering of popular questions people are asking, but let us ask the questions which people often lack the courage to face.

When the great Christian Sadhu Sundar Singh was in England, he wrote to his friends in India saying: "Pray for me, because I am desperately tempted. I would rather spend all my time in prayer than go out and fulfill my engagements." That is not an overwhelming temptation for most American preachers. But it is a temptation for American Christians, and all Christians, to stay on the sidelines rather than plunge into the midst of the battle and risk their personal welfare for the sake of the Gospel.

The early itinerant preachers of the American frontier were ready to preach at a moment's notice. In some of the records of the camp meetings of the period, we read that it was not unusual for a presiding officer to announce at the close of a late afternoon service that Brother A would preach that evening, and that was the first notice Brother A had received. Peter Cartwright said that the "western people wanted [preachers who] could mount a stump, a block, or an old log, or stand in the bed of a wagon and, without note or manuscript, quote, expound, and apply the word of God to the hearts and consciences of the people."[12]

We would not put a premium on rudeness or crudity, but those men had some sense of the living quality of their word which the scholarly preacher may very easily lose. They were preaching to "believers fighting." By all means let us study and prepare, but let not the living spirit depart from us. Perhaps one of the unnoticed virtues of the itinerant ministry was an unconscious influence in the direction of associating Christianity with movement. The early Christian preachers and apostles were usually itinerants.

It is this Gospel of action which will rescue men from despair. The man who is in pain may be given a sedative, and that will help ease the pain for the time being. Or if it is too serious a hurt, he may be given a narcotic to quiet him for a while. But you do not cure his disease that way any more than you fill the emptiness of this generation by preaching constantly about peace of mind. You had better begin to preach about purposeful action and the exciting good news which says that God is in the midst of the struggle and in the center of the crisis, calling upon each man to stand by and lend a hand. It is not hard work that kills us, but meaningless work. We need above everything else to be needed, and when men hear that God needs them

[12] Barclay, *Early American Methodism,* II, Board of Missions, 1950, 390.

in His service, amazingly enough they forget their aches and pains and cry out in gladness, "Here am I, send me."

A small boat caught in a sudden squall was behaving badly because of the helmsman's lack of skill. Then the voice of a real sailor called out: "Head her into the wind and ride her out." I heard that story at a memorial service for the late Bishop Francis J. McConnell, and it seemed to his friends that it captured his spirit. It is a necessary word for every man, for in the storms of life there is no other safety. But our good news includes the promise that one is with us on the ship who is master of the wind and the wave.

I spent an evening in the home of a layman of one of America's notable churches. This man was telling me something about a famous preacher he had listened to for many years. He said that sometimes after hearing one of that man's great sermons, he felt as if he were covered with a coat of mail which could not be penetrated by any weapon that any man might use. He said he would sometimes leave the church feeling that it would be a high honor and a great joy to lose his job, if necessary, to make a real witness for Christ. I would that men would feel that way as they left my service or as they leave yours. But I believe that if the Gospel of action is truly preached to them and the good news finds them, more times than we have dared to believe they will go from the church, not disappointed and frightened, but like warriors enlisting in the service of their Lord.

In 1881, the English revision of the New Testament was published, which was the first translation since the King James Version of 1611. It was a great event and it aroused a good deal of interest. The new version was brought to the United States by steamship and two Chicago newspapers had the idea that if it were wired to them from New York, they would have a real scoop. So the whole New Testament was telegraphed, coming in over the wire all day long. That was getting it back to its original significance—good news—something you cannot wait for—something you cannot deliver in any prosaic manner. The Gospel comes like a telegram with all the excitement of a Word that must not be delayed. Once this finds us, we shall not be in our pulpits on Sunday as lecturers to discuss some academic subject. But we shall see ourselves as God's messengers proclaiming to each man that God has acted and is acting for him, and invites every person to share in that divine activity. In the words of John Wesley, salvation is for those "who are ready for the conflict, and desire His help, and are not inactive."

III *Good News of Law*

> Think not that I have come to abolish the law and the prophets; I have come not to abolish them but to fulfil them. MATTHEW 5:17

The Gospel of Matthew reveals the influence of a man who was inclined to interpret the good news as a new law. He seems to have been familiar with the Old Testament and to have had a very deep respect for it. His mind works along orderly lines and he has a fine appreciation of the relationships between cause and effect. Jesus' teaching is organized into sermons or patterns or themes. Back of the Gospel there is the Law, and Matthew can see no real break between them. He seems to modern men to lean over backwards in finding places where the coming of Jesus was the fulfillment of the ancient prophecies. As a matter of fact, that phrase "that it might be fulfilled" occurs so often that it becomes almost wearisome. Even his baptism by John, in spite of John's reluctance, is insisted on, became "it is fitting for us to fulfill all righteousness" (3:15). So anxious is he to see similarities between the actions of Jesus and prophetic descriptions, that he finds similarities which are strained and unreal to Biblical scholars. In this he is an example of Albert Schweitzer's proposition, that no man ever gets a great idea without carrying it too far.

In Matthew, the disciple is regarded as a scribe. This gospel is concerned about the genealogy of Jesus, as if it assumed when you know about a man's background you will know something important about him. Here is a real sense of continuity and interrelatedness with the old, so that it is fitting that Matthew should be the opening book of the New Testament. Its position in the canon is due to a number of factors, but it is certainly the right book to introduce the New Testament to men who have been reading the Old Testament. It has been called "the most important book in the world" and it has been referred to as "the first book." It is hardly too much to suggest that a central theme in Matthew is the good news of law.

1. ORDERLY UNIVERSE

Every one then who hears these words of mine and does them will be like a wise man who built his house upon the rock. MATTHEW 7:24

When a modern man reads an ancient book like the *Iliad,* for example, he is shocked at the disorder assumed in that ancient world. Almost anything could happen and no man had any assurance of what would take place either in the natural world or in society. It was the whim of the gods which decided almost everything, and their jealousy of one another, or of a human being, could upset the natural processes of the world. The very foundations and framework of life seem to a modern mind to be shattered, because without the assumption that laws operate in the natural world, there seems to be no security possible and no assurance for tomorrow. We marvel that men could have any confidence in such an uncertain situation.

This makes us appreciate more than ever the great contributions science has made to civilization. We have lived with it so long that we have taken it for granted. But it is important to remember what life was like before science revealed the laws which operate constantly and inexorably in the universe. While an extreme worship of science which turned a method into a religion has wrought considerable harm in our thinking, nevertheless, we shall be wrong if we fail to understand the contribution science has made to humanity. Forest Ray Moulton put it in these words:

> From the tiny satellites in the solar system to the globular clusters, the galaxy and exterior galaxies, there is no chaos, there is nothing haphazard, and there is nothing capricious. The orderliness of the universe is the supreme discovery of science.

For one thing, it has saved us from much superstition. Man believed, previous to the age of science, that all things happening in nature were caused by spirits or gods. Now we are able to understand that things come about because of established and eternal principles which we may deal with through understanding and co-operation. It has released us from any number of foolish fears and meaningless incantations. It has undermined many a blind belief in magic and set us free.

Science has also helped to release us from fatalism. If disease was caused by evil spirits, as we thought previously, there was nothing we could do about it. But science has revealed that there is much we can do about it. The plagues which rolled over nations periodically, and came to men as the avenging spirit of God against which they were helpless, now appear to be due to natural causes, and we have learned how to combat many of them. We do not have merely to accept things as they are, but we can do a great deal to improve our situation and to make a better environment for the next generation. All of this is commonplace enough so far as most of us are concerned.

But it cannot be said too often that the gift of an orderly universe to the mind of men was one of science's great contributions and for it we must be eternally grateful. In the natural realm, it is good news indeed that the world operates on a basis of law. While at times these laws do not adjust to our convenience and we would change them if we could, nevertheless they provide the framework within which we can do our work with assurance, and make our plans with some confidence. To be released from the vagaries of the gods and to rest on natural law is one of the great steps forward that mankind has made.

But this lesson which we have learned so well in the natural world we have failed to learn in the spiritual world. We can believe in law governing atoms but we find it so difficult to believe in law affecting minds and spirits. Matthew understood that within the moral realm there is a network of eternal principles, even as there is in the natural realm. It is his experience that a new law has been revealed by Jesus and that he came to announce the principles upon which we might build our personal and social lives.

Matthew's view is one that could become legalistic and narrow. He has these words in the Sermon on the Mount, for example:

> For truly, I say to you, till heaven and earth pass away, not an iota, not a dot, will pass from the law until all is accomplished. Whoever then relaxes one of the least of these commandments

> and teaches men so, shall be called least in the kingdom of heaven; but he who does them and teaches them shall be called great in the kingdom of heaven. 5:18–19

This would have pleased the most legalistic scribe. But immediately there comes one of Jesus' most radical demands:

> For I tell you, unless your righteousness exceeds that of the scribes and Pharisees, you will never enter the kingdom of heaven. 5:20

Thus does Matthew make clear that our Lord's new law goes beyond the old and has a new spiritual inclusiveness. It operates within the framework of God's eternal love and it creates large-minded men.

Biblical criticism has been one of the most rewarding of modern studies. It has made the Bible a new book for us and has opened to us meanings which previously were hidden. But my generation of seminary students took too much delight in Biblical criticism as an end in itself. We were content to find out who wrote a certain book, why he wrote it, and the conditions under which it was written. But there was one other question which too often we left unanswered, namely, is it true? And if it is true, what is the implication for me and for my generation? After all, the important question about a thing is not who said it or when it was said or even why it was said. The important thing is to decide whether or not it speaks truth and what the implication of the truth is for us. Perhaps just now we are getting back to the realization that much Biblical criticism was more or less a clearing away of the underbrush. But to believe that we had disposed of the Bible by settling certain critical problems about it, was a great mistake. If we should follow Matthew's insight, we would say that no matter who

Jesus was or when he was born or where he was born or even how he was born, he has revealed to us the true laws of life and we had better come to terms with them. That is a place where all Christians can start.

One of the most disturbing things about our time is the number of learned men who seem to assume that a generation can play fast and loose with religion. The primary question they ask is not whether Christianity is true, but whether or not it is pleasing to the modern mind. I am growing somewhat weary of philosophers dealing with the Christian faith as if it were a mere opinion at best, and therefore to be decided for or against on the basis of the modern mood. How many times in recent days have I read these scholars in other fields who have no hesitation in dismissing Christianity for no other reason than a personal dislike, or else it has to be modified in order to fit their prejudices. If the New Testament is a new revelation of law then perhaps modern men had better come to terms with it, and if they do not, it is too bad for them. If Jesus was right, then the only choice we have is to accept him and live, or deny him and die. Surely a part of our good news is the proclamation that there are laws in the spiritual realm which were revealed in Jesus. These are the foundations upon which our lives must be built if we are to achieve our destiny and experience joy.

This highhanded pride is apparent in so many places in our time. You hear people ask how you can believe in a good God who allows war in His world. Yet the same ones who ask that question are very much irritated by the people who worship a God who denies freedom of choice to His creatures. No, they want to be free and they believe all men ought to be free, but they do not want to accept the results of their choices or to reap what their freedom sows. We cannot have it both ways, and if we are to be free men then we must accept responsibility when we do the things which bring about war. When men or nations break the laws which have been revealed to us in the New Testament, they should not be surprised if the result is suffering and death. It is a rather shabby attitude to blame God for the results of our choices and to say that He ought to save us, when our deliberate flaunting of His law brings this disaster upon our own heads. This is not to say, of course, that every man is personally responsible for war. There are too many innocent individual victims of society's sins. But let us be clear, that it is the sin of man in his wrong choices and in his denial of the moral law which brings about killing and terror. It is not God.

The same thing needs to be said about suffering. At least there is much anguish which is brought about by either our ignorance of the law or our deliberate ignoring of the law. This is not always true, of course, and I have neither the intelligence nor the space to attempt a complete facing of this problem. Thus far, at least, men must confess that they are unable to explain all the facts on the basis of a logical theory. But there is a vast amount of suffering in the world which is due to no other cause than the breaking of moral law, either by the victim himself or by his brethren. Let it be said once again that we cannot have it both ways. If we are to be free, then our evil choices will rise up and demand payment. We have no right to expect the God who created a moral universe to save us from pain when moral laws have been ignored.

Sir Winston Churchill's sixth and final volume in his important account of World War II summarizes its theme in the dedication. The words seem to describe an inescapable doom: "How the Great Democracies triumphed, and so were able to resume the follies which had so nearly cost them their life." But at the same time, he describes "the moral" of his history which is a kind of answer to the hopelessness: "In War: Resolution. In Defeat: Defiance. In Victory: Magnanimity. In Peace: Good Will." Thus, if the law is destruction when ignored, it is also security when its lessons are learned and heeded.

Moral law does not always come as judgment. It is really good news because it means that we can learn the principles by which we must live. If we follow the law, then we shall come to goodness and peace. If it is sometimes inconvenient for us to give up our desire to go in any direction our whim indicates, still if we patiently learn this lesson we know where we stand and we know what we must do if we are to be free. We are called upon to proclaim the good news of moral law.

David Dietz, Scripps-Howard science editor, accepted an invitation to deliver an annual address before an exclusive Cleveland club. He announced his subject as "Adventuring through the Universe." When the president introduced the speaker, he read a list of the distinguished speakers and their subjects at fifteen previous meetings. "In 1943," he announced, "our speaker was David Dietz and his subject—dear me—was 'Adventuring through the Universe.'" "It's the same old speech," admitted Dietz, "but you'll have to grant this too, it's the same old universe."[1] I do not advocate using the same speech, or at the very least, the same title. But it is good to know that we speak a message based on the

[1] Cerf, in *Saturday Review,* Nov. 21, 1953.

same eternal laws of God which change not, although the heavens fall.

Frederick W. Robertson, the English preacher, wrote:

> In the darkest hour through which a human soul can pass, whatever else is doubtful, this at least is certain. If there be no God and no future state, yet, even then, it is better to be generous than selfish, better to be chaste than licentious, better to be true than false, better to be brave than a coward. Blessed beyond all earthly blessedness is the man who, in the tempestuous darkness of the soul, has dared to hold fast these venerable landmarks. Thrice blessed is he who, when all is dreary and cheerless within or without, when his teachers terrify him, and his friends shrink from him, has obstinately clung to moral good.[2]

What this man saw so clearly is that underlying all our moods and impulses there is a solid foundation of law upon which we may build. Having come to terms with that, we have some protection when we face the shifting moods of an uncertain day. This is an important part of the good news which we proclaim.

2. SIGNIFICANCE OF HERITAGE

All this took place to fulfil what the Lord had spoken by the prophet. . . . MATTHEW 1:22

Our generation is in great need of appreciating the truth of heritage. We need to realize that things did not start this morning, but that most important matters began centuries ago. In any case, you do not understand the truth of an experience until you know something about what started it and from whence it has come. Popular psychology has been telling us so often in these days that life is a matter of many half-forgotten experiences, that even the man in the street

[2] Quoted by Fosdick, *A Faith for Tough Times,* Harper, 1952, 36.

should have learned it. What we are is not due only to the deliberate choices we make today but to the many fears, frustrations and choices of the past. Oftentimes the man who is healed finds health by bringing out into the open that which has been buried in his subconscious. It is not only the infant who comes trailing clouds of glory as well as clouds of despair, but every man who begins a new day. We wish to believe that we can begin each morning as if nothing had happened before, but in actual experience that is never possible. We are the inheritors of all that has gone before.

The international situation is difficult to understand for the man who has no understanding of this truth of heritage. In all sincerity, many an American fails to comprehend how the nations of the Orient can doubt us or fail to appreciate what we are trying to do for them. How is it possible to be blind to the differences between Russia and America? How can people in their right minds fail to see the superiority of democracy over communism? But what we so often forget is that the East has been on the defensive for many a year and Western civilization has been a force invading their culture. We have forgotten the arrogancy and pride which so many of our representatives showed native peoples. We do not begin with the morning headlines but with the memories which go back to the exploitation and economic tyranny, and Caucasian pride.

Nor can we understand religion as something which comes suddenly like a revelation from the mountain. It was a very wise decision on the part of the Church to refuse to separate the New Testament from the Old Testament. Marcion, who preferred a Christianity entirely divorced from its past, was quite wrong. Jesus understood this continuity so clearly that he quoted the Old Testament often and saw himself not as the beginning of a process completely new but as the fulfillment of a tradition which was very old.

Matthew was right when he understood the significance of a tradition. That God could create His saints in isolation is probably true, but that He does not do it that way is also true. The saints are part of a great tradition and we who preach the good news must never forget that. The Christian preacher is not giving only his experience and his insights, but he is bearing witness to what the prophets, the apostles, and the saints have lived and proclaimed through the years. It would be a sad thing indeed if I had to preach only the "gospel according to Kennedy," for that would be too limited and too one-sided. But through His grace, I can be the voice for those who have gone before and who have experienced heights and depths of God's love in Christ which I have never yet known. The good news of law is the good news of relationship and continuity.

This means among other things that yesterday becomes our servant. It holds us up and does not fade away. It establishes a firm footing for our endeavors in this present time. It becomes a source of power to live by and gives us confidence as we face the future. The gates of hell cannot prevail against the Church whose roots go down through nineteen hundred years of history and penetrate eternity. We are not mere historical upstarts coming to men with some new idea and some personal theory. We are witnesses of that which has been tried and tested and proved.

Education has been influenced in these days by a trend toward making great books the basis of the curriculum. We have discovered that there have been a few original contributions from which have sprung many reinterpretations year after year. The greatest of all those books is the Bible, which is the underlying foundation of our civilization and the inspiration of so much of our striving. If any man doubts the good news of heritage, let him ask himself what life would be if we could remove the Bible from our thought. It is an old book but it is the book of life for every generation.

We are surrounded by a great cloud of witnesses. We belong to the church invisible and the church triumphant. When we enter into the experience of the Sacrament of the Lord's Supper, we have again that sense of the silent but very real communion with the members who have gone before us into the other world. Every man who is a Christian finds himself surrounded by the mighty dead who are the companions of the living.

It was this understanding of the heritage that made the Apostle Paul proclaim to the Christians at Corinth:

> So let no one boast of men. For all things are yours, whether Paul or Apollos or Cephas or the world or life or death or the present or the future, all are yours; and you are Christ's; and Christ is God's. I CORINTHIANS 3:21–23

He was telling them to enter into the experience of their heritage which comes through Christ. All the great things of yesterday belong to us precisely because we belong to Christ and Christ belongs to God. This is the good news of law which means the good news of heritage.

3. OBLIGATION AND RESPONSIBILITY

> My Father, if this cannot pass unless I drink it, thy will be done. MATTHEW 26:42

The generation that has not accepted the good news of law soon loses its sense of obligation. This is one of the most general characteristics of our time. Our life is influenced by a kind of rootlessness which recognizes no debt to the past and no obligation to the future. We take what is offered without much thought of passing it on to the next generation. Nor do we feel any great sense of thankfulness to those who bequeathed these gifts to us. My own life is in some ways an illustration of this contemporary tendency. I have never lived in any one place very long, partly due to the fact that I have been a Methodist preacher. But even in my childhood we moved a good deal. The longest time we ever lived in one city was six years and during the six years we moved four times. My father had a strange feeling that it was immoral to stay in any one place very long. He was a great believer in John Wesley's admonition that men ought not to remain in one locality any longer than was absolutely necessary. I find myself going into a city and accepting all the things which the city affords without consideration of the pioneers who made these gifts possible for me. I have found it necessary to take thought of the past and recognize that because I have received so much, I must do something to improve the city for the next generation.

Some years ago the English novelist, J. B. Priestley, came to the Southwest for the winter. While he spent most of his time in Arizona, he lived part of the winter in Southern California. He said he had a feeling of the impermanence of the country, as if the cities were really a kind of de luxe camping. He expected to wake up any morning and find that the whole population had moved on somewhere else, and even the hills might be rolled up like brown bearskin rugs. The thousands of people who continue to come into this section of the country seem to have an idea of permanence, but what he sensed was this modern atmosphere of change which seemed accentuated in this particular place.

The willingness of too many people to assassinate the characters of individuals with whom they disagree is indicative of this same tendency. No man with any profound sense of his obligation and responsibility to the past and to the future could throw epithets around so loosely as some American public figures have been doing. We ought to remember the experience of Rome which was far along on the road to decay when the public servants denied their responsibility to the society which they were supposed to serve. A man who is willing to sow distrust and suspicion among his brethren for the sake of headlines and political notice is a notorious example of the kind of man who represents the disease of our day.

My job makes it necessary for me to travel East on the train several times each year. Sometimes the railroad goes along beside the old Oregon Trail where the pioneers traveled westward a generation or two ago. There are places in western Nebraska where I have walked in the ruts of the old wagon wheels. As I sit in a comfortable, air-conditioned roomette and travel down the rails seventy-five miles an hour, my imagination can see the prairie schooners rocking on their way painfully and slowly a few miles each day. And it comes to me that if they had not made the trip the hard way I could not be making it the easy way. I am the recipient of gifts created out of their courage, their sacrifice, their vision.

Remember St. Paul's fine words, "I am a debtor." No man enters into his true heritage as a son of God until he realizes this truth of obligation. But this is good news, for it rescues men from their isolationism and their unrelatedness, and makes them realize that they belong to a mighty fellowship of the past. It is ennobling to recognize that we are obligated to pay our debt through service to the future. Evelyn Underhill put it this way: "In Revelation it is the saints and elders nearest God who cast down their crowns when they adore him. The lesser fry, further off, are quite content to go on wearing theirs."[3] When men catch a vision of all they have received, they enter into their true inheritance and accept their obligation and responsibility. This is another part of the good news of law.

Men often resent the burden of obligation and duty, and see their release from hard demands as the attainment of happiness. It is hardly ever true that such escape means contentment. The loss of the tension leaves us unstrung and confused. We are like Edward Gibbon who, when he came to the end of the long and arduous labor connected with writing *The Decline and Fall of the Roman Empire,* laid it down and walked out into his garden. At first he felt a wonderful sense of release, and then he writes in his memoirs: "But my pride was soon humbled and a sober melancholy was spread over my mind by the idea that I had taken an everlasting leave of an old and agreeable companion." Law is our taskmaster, but it is also our good companion.

Our Lord has set us a perfect example of one who accepted the obligation and responsibility to do the will of God wherever it might lead him. He lived his life within the framework of that will, and humbled himself to fulfill his Messiah's role of suffering. Thus he prays in the garden, that the agony facing him may be taken away. But when the answer to his prayer is no, he moves forward toward the inevitable crucifixion to die for those who know not what they do. It is this acceptance of an obligation to people who had proved worthy of no sacrifice on his part that humbles the pride of all men who accept him as Saviour.

This is one of the great differences between Jesus and the other conquerors. Hitler, in the name of creating a Reich that would last a thousand years and make him the tyrant

[3] Quoted by Day, *op. cit.*, 55.

of the whole world, threw the moral law aside, sought the annihilation of Christianity, and ridiculed any concept of responsibility for the weak or the humble. Karl Marx dreamed of supplanting one class with another, and his followers have no hesitancy in liquidating those who stand in the way of the dictatorship of the proletariat. But Jesus said, "I came not to destroy but to fulfill."

The saints have understood always that only by following this path of responsibility can they expect to come to peace and joy. St. Francis prayed that he might be an instrument of God's peace. The author of Hebrews linked his generation up with the long processes of God in these words:

> And all these, though well attested by their faith, did not receive what was promised, since God had foreseen something better for us, that apart from us they should not be made perfect.
> HEBREWS 11:39–40

Even as past generations depended upon the present, so only future generations will fulfill our dreams or hopes, if they are to attain fulfillment.

If the law has its limitations, it has important contributions to make to our lives. Professor G. B. Caird speaks of three main functions it fulfills.

> It provides an orderly social framework within which the gospel can be preached and can do its work. It leads men to repentance; for those who seriously attempt to fufill the demands of law, duty, and conscience, find that they cannot do so without such help as Christ offers through the gospel. And it is the schoolhouse of character in which our unruly impulses are disciplined for the responsibilities of freedom."[4]

Paul DeKruif was discussing with a young man how

[4] Caird, *The Truth of the Gospel,* Oxford, 1950, 143.

gentle and kindly most of the great scientists had seemed to be. Yet they were the ones who finally produced the A-bomb. They had seemed like innocent magicians, perhaps like the old medieval sorcerer who had worked out the secret of creating water out of nothing. When the old wizard was away his apprentice found the secret formula and turned it on but did not know how to turn it off. If the old man had not returned, the world would have been flooded. Then said the young man, "Of course, it isn't the scientist's fault. What we have now is just scientific curiosity—perverted." But DeKruif replied, "What we've got now is irresponsibility." [5]

There seems to be a law of life, that until men come to terms with their responsibility, whoever they may be, no decent life is possible for any of us. Over against this spirit of selfish unconcern, we may look at a monument which was unveiled in Norway after the war, and on it was inscribed only one word: No! It was raised in honor of the martyrs of the resistance movement during the Nazi occupation. Part of our good news is that men are responsible and men are obligated and they find their personal fulfillment in obedience to this law. If it is a hard saying which we have to proclaim, it is also the word of the discipline upon which must rest our freedom and fulfillment of our destiny.

4. FOR THE PREACHER

. . . for he taught them as one who had authority, and not as their scribes. MATTHEW 7:29

The preacher may fall into the trap of considering himself a salesman for a particular brand of philosophy. The modern pulpit sometimes impresses us as simply another propaganda center in a society that is already surfeited with

[5] DeKruif, *Life among the Doctors,* Harcourt, Brace, 1949, 302.

propaganda. It has become a commonplace to regard the preacher as one who approaches his victims from the blind side in the attempt to unload his product upon them after he has broken down their resistance. A woman who had spent the day with an old friend came home in the evening and said to her husband, "I have had the most wonderful day today. Neither of us tried to prove anything to the other." I think she meant that it is good for people to share the truth of their experiences without any attempt to assault the mind of the other with argument or pressure.

The pulpit needs to have this calm, assumed sense of authority which comes with the realization that because the message is rooted in the laws of life, it is true. The hurried, nervous, high-powered approach of the modern preacher who has become imbued with a success philosophy is a denial not only of the dignity of our high calling, but of its reality. The prophet does not argue but he proclaims. So the man who is proclaiming the judgment of God and announcing His will for men ought to have something of the authority and objectivity of a judge. We are not the spokesman of One who is seeking clients, but we are witnesses for One who has revealed truth.

There are preachers whose approach resembles that of a district attorney who will be coming up for election next year. They seem to feel that their whole record is at stake and they must get so many convictions to their credit, no matter how the convictions may be obtained. Proudly they announce the number of new members or the size of the budget or the prominent leaders they have ensnared. Perhaps we can take a leaf from our English brethren who hold the attitude that "the Crown cannot win and the Crown cannot lose." They mean that the task of the public prosecutor is not to get convictions but to establish justice. He does not announce publicly the number of convictions he has to his credit, for that is not his aim. It is unthinkable that a British prosecutor should fail to turn over to the defense any important evidence, nor can he hide any witness favorable to the defendant. Let the preacher rest back upon the quiet confidence that his case is not to be won by argument, but by setting forth God's truth in Christ.

The good news of law means for the preacher also that his work must rest on a foundation of discipline. There are too many sermons with flashes of greatness here and there, interspersed with dull periods full of the sound of a mighty rushing wind but no still, small voice. One of my best friends was a member of a church where one of my classmates was pastor. He told me that going to church Sunday morning was one of the most frustrating experiences he had ever had. Every now and again this man would begin his sermon with great promise, and my friend would sit back with the assurance that today he was to be fed spiritually. Then something would come to the preacher's mind and he would start off on a tangent and seem to lose himself on some side path. At the end he might come back to the thought with another flash of insight. But the worse the sermon, the longer it lasted. My friend told me that what made him most unhappy was the realization that here was a man who had the gifts of the preacher if he could have learned the discipline to make the gifts effective.

We have all known preachers who were either very good or very bad. Catch them at a high point, and one would say that there are few men in the country who were ever better. Listen to them the next time, and they might be so bad you were ashamed for them. These are the brethren with the natural gifts of expression who have yielded to the temptation to depend upon the inspiration of the moment. Or they have allowed their sermon preparation to become secondary to the rest of the program. It is impossible for any man, I should think, to be at his best every time he stands in the pulpit. No matter how hard we work there will be times when we will reach the heights, and other times when the wings refuse to carry us aloft. But there is a level of excellence below which no man needs to sink, and it is never necessary for his friends to be ashamed of him. All of this, however, means that underneath the grace of expression there has to be the law of organization. The good news of law for the preacher proclaims that if he will do his work faithfully and follow the disciplines of his craft, God will always find him a useful servant.

It is too bad that a man may discover early in his ministry that emotionalism can be used to cover over a lack of thought. I doubt that any preacher has not discovered that a sob story properly told can blind the majority of the congregation to the inadequacy of his preparation and the shallowness of his discourse. As John Ruskin once said, we are so often admired for the worst parts of our sermons. It is not to be wondered at, therefore, if men fall back on a clever manipulation of the emotions as a substitute for real preaching. But let us realize at the beginning that if a man's mind has not been changed, a temporary mood will have no lasting effect. As one of Nathaniel Burton's deacons said, when asked about calling in an emotional evangelist, "This is a very poor community to cry in." Preachers ought to weep with those who weep; but tears as a substitute for intellectual discipline get very monotonous.

It is said that DeQuincy never tidied up his room but allowed it to get so cluttered and dirty that he could stand it no longer himself. Then he would take refuge in morphine, and after it became impossible to live in the room any longer even under that condition, he moved somewhere else. All through his life, for a period of thirty-seven years, he moved from room to room, leaving behind I do not know how many dirty and cluttered-up places for someone else to clean.

Unfortunately there are preachers like that. Their slovenly habits of preparation allow them to fill a pulpit for a time, but soon they must leave for a fresh start. They leave behind them a pastoral untidiness for their successors to clean up. They wonder why their ministries become shorter instead of longer, and they consider themselves badly treated because other men are in demand and they are not. It is true that the great preacher has a gift which is given, but it is also true—and this is good news—that every preacher has gifts which, if they are trained and disciplined, will give him a sense of growth and development with the passing years.

As a matter of fact, the years should bring fulfillment to every preacher. I am more aware now than ever before of the church's unseemly desire for young preachers. This is something hard to understand. For other things being equal, the man who has been in the ministry for twenty-five years ought to be a much better preacher and pastor than the man who has just come from seminary. When one imagines the kind of message a man rich in pastoral experience and wise from many acquaintances can deliver, as compared with the man who is merely at the beginning, one wonders why the church does not prefer the older preacher.

The answer is not far to seek. Too many of us do not find our ministries expanding with the passing years, but contracting and getting weaker. If one might paraphrase a line from a song made popular by a returning general some years ago, "Old preachers never die, they just fade away." Because of this frequent tendency, most church committees would rather risk the young man, who having just come out of school ought to have some fresh material which will last him for a few years at least.

Yet this is not necessary, and there are men whose gathering years have simply increased their ability and power. Some time ago Harry Emerson Fosdick came to the Pacific School of Religion to give the Earl Lectures. I found it impossible to attend, much to my regret. But about thirty-five of the Methodist ministers in my Portland Area did attend, and when they came back they told me about them. Most of the men who went were the younger, more critical preachers, and I wondered how even Dr. Fosdick would fare. To my delight, I did not hear one sour note nor one adverse criticism. Man after man said to me, "He is better than ever." Few things have happened that so lifted up my heart, because it said to me that after a man retires from his active ministry, he may still grow and find increasing fulfillment in his service. The heritage of our own past and the years of our previous preparation all belong to us, and if we do not rest on that heritage, but use it as a goad to press us forward, the best is yet to be.

We are all the inheritors of a great profession. We stand upon the shoulders of the preachers of yesterday, as well as upon the insights of our own past experiences and the increasing richness of our personal relations and spiritual discoveries. The good news of law for the preacher means among other things that he may expect increasing delight in his work with every passing year, if he accepts the discipline of hard work and obeys the laws of preparation.

One of the leaders of the Evangelical Movement in Germany was Klaus Harms. When he was seventy-five years old, he was asked to speak at a seminar for preachers and discuss the importance of preparation and study. After his lecture was over, one young man objected and said that the Holy Spirit would give a man words to speak in the pulpit, and that for a man to prepare, as had been suggested, was to show a lack of faith in the Spirit. Whereupon Dr. Harms replied that he had been preaching for fifty years, and in all that time he could not remember that the Holy Spirit spoke to him directly in the pulpit more than twice. "But," he said, "the spirit often spoke to me when I left the pulpit, and what he said was 'Klaus, you have been lazy.'" The joy of the Gospel which the saints have experienced, and the glory which comes to the man who feels that he has delivered his soul to the best of his ability, are experiences which rest back upon the disciplines of the spiritual life. The good news which many a frustrated preacher needs to hear is the good news of law. For if it is exacting and demanding, it contains also the promises of freedom, assurance, and enlarging fulfillment.

IV *Good News of Concern*

> But while he was yet at a distance, his father saw him and had compassion. . . . LUKE 15:20

The Gospel of Luke proclaims Jesus' universal concern for all men and his particular interest in the disinherited of the world. His genealogy begins not with Abraham but with Adam, the progenitor of the whole race, and the concern of our Lord is not for his own countrymen alone, but for all people. He is the friend of the poor and the unfortunate. He understands the problems of men disregarded by their communities and given the lowly jobs of the world to do. The Gospel of Luke is good news to these people, for it is the story of one who comes to bring the assurance that God takes thought for every person, regardless of his status. This is a prophetic book which judges the standards of our life and finds them false. It is a proclamation that God looks upon men from the point of view of an eternal love.

There is discernible in Luke a tendency to soften the picture of men's motives and actions. Sometimes he leaves out stories which place men in a bad light, though the other Gospels include them. The disciples are excused for their dullness and misunderstandings because they are weary or confused. In the Garden, Matthew and Mark state bluntly that the disciples fell asleep, but Luke says that they were "sleeping for sorrow" (22:45). Even the enemies of Jesus receive a gentler treatment in this Gospel.

A generation that glories in black pictures as the essence of "realism" may dismiss this tendency as unhistorical and sentimental. But the man who approaches his brethren with sympathy must be uncertain many times when he tries to place a judgment on their real qualities. At any rate, Luke thought that his Master would have leaned in the direction of a kindly tenderness. The Gospel of Luke exhibits in all personal relationships "the grace of our Lord Jesus Christ."

This is not a document of the class war, as some have interpreted it. It does not suggest that there is a particular virtue in the poor which makes it necessary for them to supplant the rich, but it is so direct in its description of the unlovely traits of the rich and proud that it has a revolutionary tone. It is the assurance that every man is equally precious in the eyes of God and that He has no patience with our artificial divisions. It is an insistence that through the humble He can reveal himself best, and He comes to the proud as judgment and destruction. But to every person who has been beaten down by life, this good news comes to assure him of rehabilitation and release. If we should characterize briefly one of the most beautiful books ever written, we might say that it is pre-eminently the good news of a divine concern for every man.

1. THE COMING OF JESUS

. . . therefore the child to be born will be called holy, the Son of God. LUKE 1:35

There are so few atheists in the world because it takes more credulity to accept the atheistic position than most men can muster. Those who make many thoughtful observations of this world, and consider the variety and meaning of their experiences, usually come to a theistic faith which can hardly ever be denied. Human experience and the world mean something, and this implies a divine intelligence. Men in their despair and agony may curse God. But like Swinburne, who sometimes complains bitterly and ridicules Him, they will be impelled like the poet to express their wonder, awe, and praise as they stand in the presence of some unmistakable sign of the glory of God. A small boy asked an old man if it was possible to see God, and he replied, "My boy, as I grow older I find it impossible to look anywhere in this world of His without seeing God." For myself, I marvel that any man with any perception whatsoever can live very many years without being convinced of the reality of God.

The power to respond to the world's beauty, which the great naturalists and the nature poets have in abundance, each man has to some extent. It may be the grandeur of the Grand Canyon or it may be the twilight in a little town. But to most of us there come those quiet moments when we cannot doubt that the world is full of an ineffable presence. Each man grows especially fond of the country he calls his own, so it may be forgiven me if I suggest that any man who travels around Southern California, Arizona, and the Hawaiian Islands is blessed far beyond his deserving. He can go nowhere without having his heart lifted up by the beauty of the Islands, the desert, the mountains. If a man has within him even a small appreciation of beauty, he can hardly escape the feeling that the One who creates it must be worthy of his worship.

Or he may turn to the records of history and read what men have put down as worthy of remembering. No matter what school of history the writer may have belonged to, his story can hardly fail to have overtones of purpose and undertones of moral reality. There is unmistakably a more than human power making for righteousness, and in the long run it is well with the good and ill with the evil, as James Anthony Froude said. It does not seem to me that history is merely a record of God's championing of the big battalions. On the contrary, it seems to me that He is on the side of the strong and true convictions, as Bishop Westcott observed. Is it not true that history seems to be the story of the comparative weakness of sheer brute power and the incomparable might of the spiritual things which are unseen? Even the great disasters are signs of His judgment and the essential trustworthiness of His promises which stand revealed when things go wrong. Thus in the apocalyptic section of the Gospels a description is given of the devastation which men may expect in the days ahead. But this coming catastrophe is not to be regarded as mere accident or as a destruction wrought by blind forces which have no moral purposes. These debacles are necessary because they establish the knowledge of God's government and the futility of denying God's will. They have within them therefore an element of hope and assurance, and Luke has a rather unusual but wonderful word at the end of the section describing the disasters which must overtake the nations. He writes, "Now when these things begin to take place, look up and raise your heads, because your redemption is drawing near" (Luke 21:28). It is as if he were saying that these things too should be regarded as evidence of God.

The universe, with its marvel of organization, harmony,

and balance, cannot be explained on any theory of chance or mathematical probability. The very nature of the universe and its construction keep bringing new demands that men believe in God. It is noteworthy that a philosopher like Walter T. Stace of Princeton University, while critical and somewhat skeptical concerning the Christian faith, still takes great delight in showing the untrustworthy nature of modern skepticism and doubt. If we take Jesus' word that he who is not against us is for us, then such men may be nearer the Kingdom of God than even they realize. No, the problem of religion is not atheism. The external evidence and the inner assurance unite to make it a relatively harmless opponent of religion.

But the real problem is whether God has any real concern for an individual. Our minds express the question of the little girl who gave the opening of the Lord's Prayer this significant interpretation: "Our Father, who art in heaven, How do you know my name?" Does He know my name and is He interested at all in the affairs which seem important to me, even though I must be the first to confess that they have no universal significance? Is God available to the man whose heart is broken or who has descended to the depths of failure and despair? For while I may believe that nature reveals God and that history shows His presence in the rise and fall of the nations, or even that the universe is proof of divine mind back of it and in it, still all of this is not enough for me. Where do I find power enough to live by, and where can I discover the cleansing of my sin?

In the seventh chapter of the Book of Numbers there is a story of the leaders of the tribes coming to Moses and presenting to him six covered wagons, each wagon drawn by two oxen. These were distributed among the tribes according to their service in the tabernacle. Then in the ninth verse of the seventh chapter there is this interesting note: "But to the sons of Kohath he gave none, because they were charged with the care of the holy things which had to be carried on the shoulder." It was a true insight that you can use wagons to carry things of bulk, material things especially, but when it comes to the holy things and the sacred things of life, they must be carried personally, individually, on men's shoulders.

In this we have a foretaste of the Incarnation. For Christianity insists that in the coming of Jesus, God came to take upon His shoulders the sins and sufferings of every man. It is a revelation that not only does the universe rest on moral laws, but that God's eye is on the sparrow and on me. He did not send me a message from afar off, nor did He seek to deal with men in the bulk. He came Himself to a Cross and a grave, that men might experience the redemption of a divine concern that was personal. Not only is God to be found in nature, in history, and in the universe, but in the words of St. Paul, "God was in Christ reconciling the world to himself. . . ." (II Corinthians 5:19). This becomes not just a general concern for the race and its destiny, but an experience of God's love that redeems persons.

E. B. White points out that Clarence Day was hardly noticed when he wrote his *Thoughts without Words,* which was his best writing. But when he brought his father to life, he became generally loved and known. White adds: ". . . don't write about man, write about *a* man."[1] Do you see how this says something important about God's word in Jesus? This is, of course, the center of the good news.

A neighbor woman asked a young doctor to take her sick

[1] White, *The Second Tree from the Corner,* Harper, 1954, 178.

cat away and get rid of it. He took it and killed it instantly before her eyes. He did not say anything to her but his action said that if one wants to get rid of something unpleasant then he ought to look at the consequences of the wish.[2] So it was that Jesus came to bear in his own life the cruelty which springs from the sin of men that God hates. This is what theologians have tried to make clear when they described God taking unto Himself the burdens of our evil. It has been that startling word which for nineteen hundred years has brought men to the foot of the Cross, where for the first time they could begin to appreciate the meaning of the good news.

That Jesus had perfect confidence in his Father's love and protection cannot be doubted. It shines through all his teaching and it undergirds all his life. But more than that, he settled the doubts of his followers on this question. There is something about Jesus which carries a conviction that the eternal God is our personal refuge and safety. This, I take it, is what Christians have meant when they talked about Jesus bringing God near to us. Through His care of our Lord, we experience His care for us.

Some years ago there was a condemned murderer serving a life sentence in Sing Sing prison. A little girl had been stricken with the cancerous disease of the blood called leukemia. It was still hoped that if she could receive enough healthy blood her life might be saved, though there was no assurance of it. But it could not be done by giving the blood through a tube. It must be vein to vein, which meant that some of her diseased blood might infect the donor. But this man volunteered. In some small way, that is what Christians have been trying to say when they talked about being

[2] DeKruif, *op. cit.*, 23.

saved by the blood of Jesus. He did not send it to us from afar off but came to heal us vein to vein. And while we sometimes blur our theological definitions, the essential Christian experience is that God in Christ assures each man that the divine concern is so real that the King of kings has suffered with him and died for him.

Henry Sloane Coffin relates that he one time asked a group of Chinese pastors in an interior town what there was in Christ that had impressed them the most. None of them mentioned any of the miracles, for the mythologies of other religions could outdo the marvels recorded in the Gospel. Various replies were suggested but finally one elderly man said, "His washing his disciples' feet," and suddenly they all seemed to realize that this was it. That the Son of God should take the place of the lowliest slave had won their allegiance and redeemed their lives.[3] This is not only good news, it is the best news that any man was commissioned to proclaim. In all of our preaching, we must never get very far away from this central doctrine of our Gospel. The sermon which does not have within it some word, direct or implied, about the Incarnation, has been found lacking in one of the essential elements of Christian preaching.

2. IMPLICATIONS FOR CHRISTIANS

Today salvation has come to this house, since he also is a son of Abraham. LUKE 19:9

The success of our materialistic civilization has so influenced us that even Christians have missed the way. We have done too much in the materialistic realm and left undone those weightier matters of the spirit. Our confidence has been in physical security and in the hope that inner fear

[3] Jones, *op. cit.*, 158.

would flee from men who had built the larger barns for their many possessions. One can get sentimental and unrealistic about poverty and all of us will understand the man who said, "I've been rich and poor. Rich is better." We do not need to despise the high aim of a civilization which hopes to make every family's standard of living adequate, but every minister knows that most unhappy people have troubles which are not subject to materialistic solutions at all. Perhaps one of the first great discoveries which comes to a young preacher is the realization that happiness so seldom has much relation to the bank account. Men do not live by bread alone any more in the twentieth century than they did in the first century.

The possessions which we gain too often make us suspicious and fearful of any social change, rather than set us free. A friend of mine said not long ago that in his judgment it was not too hard to make money if you did not care how you made it. I think that is probably true. But the closed mind and the reactionary attitudes which cause men of great possessions to tremble before the suggestion of more equality which may in any small way cut down their profits, are some of the most distressing things to observe. That there are some wonderful exceptions to this every person must know from his own acquaintances. But that possessions can enslave the spirit and destroy the soul is all too obvious.

This inordinate concern with possessions has led us to depersonalize our society. We begin to think that we can deal with people in terms of bulk rather than in terms of personal relationships. Propaganda takes the place of information, and the very concept of propaganda is depersonalizing. For it implies that men are not to be dealt with as men, but as a mass which can be manipulated and brought to acquiescence by spending enough money to tell enough people the same thing enough times. The danger of communism in America is small if we mean an actual substitution of that economic and political system for the democratic way we hold. But it may win a subtle victory over our minds if it makes us think not in terms of citizens but in terms of masses.

Our charity becomes too often a mechanical thing far removed from the persons it is supposed to serve. The community chest movement in our big cities seems to be necessary, and I have worked on chest drives and in chest organizations for many years. It bothers me considerably, however, to know how many of our citizens after they have been pressured, even politely blackmailed, write out their check for agencies they have no knowledge of and for which they feel no real concern. They have been persuaded they must do it since other people are doing it. But it is the kind of charity which does not warm the heart nor stir the sympathy, but merely creates an unloving smugness. This is the kind of human relationship which does not help the giver and has too little effect upon the receiver.

The supposition that men must have good done to them by wise, well-meaning bureaucrats is a popular fetish which experience repudiates. There is a story of a Communist agitator proclaiming from his soapbox that after the revolution everyone would have strawberries and cream every meal. "But Comrade," protested one poor listener, "I do not like strawberries and cream." "Comes the revolution," replied the speaker fiercely, "you get strawberries and cream." A Methodist missionary to Cuba had to eat a dish of cold oatmeal without cream or sugar and act as if he enjoyed it because a well-meaning family had heard that Americans liked oatmeal, and they had prepared it as a special delicacy for their guest. Generous actions without personal knowledge and planned charity for the masses usually misfire.

We have been generous in sending food and munitions to our allies, but we wonder why it is that these things seem to accomplish so little in terms of better international relationships. Why do they not appreciate it more and express that appreciation by doing what we ask them to do? No nation has been more generous than America during these past years, but somehow the unity which we might expect to grow out of this generosity has not materialized.

Governments would do well to learn something from the Christian missionary enterprise. The Christian family that goes to the faraway land and lives there accomplishes more for peace than a hundred diplomats. For men are influenced by persons and they are saved by establishing right human relationships. The gift in itself is not enough but it must be accompanied by the concern of the giver. Jesus never generalized these matters but always insisted that we must go directly to the man we would love. It is one man who gives a cup of cold water in his name who shall receive the reward. It is one good Samaritan doing good to the one man who had fallen among the thieves. You may say that conditions were much different then from what they are now. In some ways of course that is true, although I do not think they were as different as we sometimes assume. But the principle remains eternally the same. When societies get depersonalized and the word "neighbor" loses its meaning, the sickness of isolationism and selfishness deteriorates character and contaminates the source of our common welfare.

Man is a spirit and the values which are essential for his life are all spiritual. He must have self-respect, which can neither be given nor taken away by economic success or failure. He must have freedom, which can never be purchased. He must have character, which has nothing whatsoever to do with his social status. He must have the respect of his brethren, which is never for sale. This is where so much of our modern social work has gone astray. It has been based upon the assumption that men are concerned only with food and shelter, and that a society can protect itself by providing these things for its citizens. This is not true and while food and shelter must be provided for the people who need it, the problem is not solved until men have had restored their dignity, their worth, and their value.

A man spent several weeks in a transient camp in California and gave account of his experiences there and the kind of people he met.[4] He found them to be men who had not held jobs and probably would not hold regular jobs very long even if they were provided. He felt that they were not below the average intellectually, and it came to him suddenly that probably they were the kind of men who had been the pioneers. Not very happy at home and having no steady job and little to hold them there, they had been willing to try the desert, and the plains, and the mountains. He talked to some of the old-timers who had known the Forty-niners of California, and asked them which men in the present generation they most resembled. After they had thought about it for a little while, they came to the conclusion that the fruit tramps most clearly resembled the pioneers. This led to the startling idea that not only the superior individuals but the ordinary men in every generation play the significant parts. And as Hoffer's imagination

[4] Hoffer, "The Role of the Undesirables," *Harper's Magazine,* Dec., 1952.

saw this vast continent waiting to be tamed and exploited for human use, he writes:

> And the lowly were not awed by the magnitude of the task. A hunger for action, penned up for centuries, found an outlet. They went to it with axe, pick, shovel, plough, and rifles; on foot, on horses, in wagons and on flat boats. . . . This is how I read the statement that this country was built by hordes of undesirables from the Old World.

We must remember that it was these so-called "undesirables" that Jesus called and enlisted in the greatest of all enterprises, the building of the Christian church.

We need to come back to a realization of the importance of every personal relationship and every personal deed. When I drive down to my office in the morning and have to turn left at a very busy intersection, every now and again someone will stop and wave me across. I must confess this does not take place too often. But whenever it does happen, it makes me feel better all day long because someone has done a courteous thing—someone upon whom I had no claim made way for my convenience. The contrary truth is that an undeserved and unexpected act of discourtesy and rudeness will make me feel cast down for a long time after I have forgotten the actual cause of my gloom. Even in this highly industrialized society of ours, I suspect that if we knew the truth, many times a small act has been responsible for nobility or tragedy, for success or failure. Our world is full of lonely people to whom a simple kindness is more important than any material gift which might be given them.

I remember reading a novel many years ago (the author and title I have forgotten) whose plot consisted in tracing the effect of the birth of a baby on the lives of a number of people. Because the baby was born, it had an effect on another person and he in turn reacted on another, until that one event had sent its influence into a score of lives and profoundly effected a number of important events. Let no Christian man play down his influence and the significance of it. Let none of us get lost in the mass movements of our time, but in every situation let us bring the healing of our personal concern.

I am impressed with the number of men whose most treasured memories are of individual acts of kindness. Talk to a man on the train and he will tell you of a missionary aunt who practiced her religion, or a mother who was the incarnation of virtue. He will talk about a friend who did him an unexpected kindness. His life seems to consist of innumerable small deeds done and a host of never-to-be-forgotten personal relationships.

A few years ago as a member of the American Seminar under the direction of Sherwood Eddy, I listened to James Mallon of Toynbee Hall relate the beginnings of that institution. It was one of the earliest and most famous of the social settlements and for a number of years it has been a center of hope and regeneration in London's East End. Toynbee Hall was begun by a minister, who came to the conclusion that if you were going to help people you could not do it from a distance. He despised the kind of people who went slumming occasionally and then scurried back to their own comfortable homes. So he went down to the East End to live with the people, and he brought there from time to time some of the bright young men of Cambridge and Oxford to give a period of their lives in service to these neglected and forgotten ones. We do not help people very much from a distance, and if we are to follow in the footsteps of our Lord, we shall know that it is necessary for us to be the personal messengers and incarnations of concern.

3. THE RESPONSIBILITY OF THE CHURCH

But he said to them, "You give them something to eat." LUKE 9:13

A man sat in a Protestant church service one Sunday with his hat on. After a while an usher came to him and said, "We do not wear hats in our service here." "I know it," replied the man, "but I have been coming here for over a year and decided I would do something to make somebody speak to me." This may be an exaggeration, but there are churches where people act as if they were in some exclusive club where every stranger must be made to feel ill at ease and unwelcome. It is true that in too many church services there is no personal feeling among the members worthy of the name of fellowship. The only relationship is between the pulpit and the pew, and it consists of nothing more than a routine greeting which the minister gives those individuals who care to stand in line when the service is over.

There are a few people who feel no lack in an impersonal worship service. I remember a man in one of my churches who always came in just before the sermon and left immediately upon its conclusion. He was a rather eccentric professor who said to me one time that I was not to be troubled by his rather strange behavior. He said that he did not like to sing hymns, he was not particularly interested in hearing the scripture read, and he was usually bored by the prayer. So far as the offering was concerned, I could forget it, because he would send the church a check once each year according to how much he thought the sermon was worth to him personally. (I never dared to inquire about the size of the check.) But for every man like that, there are a hundred who are in deep need of experiencing the fellowship of the church.

John Wesley declared that the Christian religion "is essentially a social religion, and . . . to turn it into solitary religion is indeed to destroy it." He was very emphatic upon this point and he says in another place:

> The gospel of Christ knows of no religion, but social; no holiness but social holiness. Faith working by love is the length and breadth and depth and height of Christian perfection. This commandment have we from Christ, that he who loves God will love his brother also; and that we manifest our love by doing good unto all men, especially to them that are of the household of faith.[5]

One of the great faults of the American church is a tendency to substitute organization for vital Christian fellowship. One who sees how churches in other countries fail to take advantage of their opportunities to establish youth work and develop educational programs will not desire to minimize what the American church is doing in these fields. So far as activity and vitality are concerned, American Christianity has no rival.

A man cannot preach in the great churches of America or learn something about their programs without being thrilled by the all-inclusiveness of the American Protestant interpretation of the Gospel. There is something spectacular and inspiring about an organization which has thousands of members and a budget of several hundred thousand dollars each year. But we must wonder sometimes why we make such a relatively small impact on our society.

The church of the New Testament had none of these

[5] Quoted by Barclay, *op. cit.*, I, 1949, p. xxviii.

things, but it did have something much more precious. It had a sense of the oneness of men in Christ. It was a place where men experienced friendship with one another because they were united in a common Christian task and facing up to it in the midst of danger. The church was then, and is now when it is at its best, the greatest fellowship in the world. It cuts across all lines of class, race, and sex. It is universal in its scope and it touches life at its deepest place as it confronts the most serious issues. We cannot have the church at its best unless we have Christian fellowship in its widest, fullest, and most complete reality.

It would be wise for ministers and laymen to analyze the programs of their churches every year to see if it is possible for any person to be neglected or forgotten. Our cities and towns are full of unhappy people who are seeking desperately and pathetically for the answer to their loneliness. It is a tragic and sad thing when any man enters a Christian church and leaves feeling as lonely as he came. Yet this is not only possible, but it is the general experience of many people every Sunday. Too often they sit in a congregation and find each member concerned with his own family and his own friends, and because they have neither, they never are brought into the circle. The church can be interested in Man and neglect men. I have no doubt that it would be a most disturbing knowledge if we learned how many people came seeking the fellowship the true church should give, and left having failed to find it. Rotary Clubs often do a much better job.

If you talk with a first-rate psychiatrist these days, you will discover that underneath his professional objectivity he is disturbed by the number of people who are heading for mental institutions. It may be that more serious than the threat of communism or the threat of outside military attack is the threat of mental instability within our own society. Never was there a time when the church could perform such a valuable function as just now. For men are healed when they are related to one another in terms of love and concern. They disintegrate when they are cast aside. The good news of concern is the message of the church, but it is preached best, not from the pulpit but through a demonstration within its own fellowship.

Charles Tudor Leber relates that in 1942 he landed in the Cameroons, West Africa. He was invited to preach through an interpreter to a Bulu Christian congregation. In a large church building back in a jungle clearing, four thousand people came to the service. What could a man say to these half-clothed Africans deep in the bush? He decided he would give them a brief devotional talk with several personal illustrations. When the preaching service was over, a tall, dark Bulu arose and prayed passionately. Dr. Leber asked what he was praying about and the interpreter replied, "He is praying for the Christians in China, in Japan, in Germany, in Russia, in America; praying that they will be true in their hour of testing, and that in the trials of faith the African Christians will be courageous and faithful too."[6] One could find no better illustration of what the Christian ecumenical movement is and what it ought to be. We are united around the world with our brethren in every country and on every continent in terms of love and Christian concern.

I shall not forget the meeting of the Central German Conference of the Methodist Church in 1953. As the pastors

[6] Leber, *op. cit.*, 38.

and laymen gathered together at the seminary in Frankfurt to elect a bishop, their brethren from the Eastern Zone were absent, having been refused permission to come to the Conference. But when one of the leaders of that Conference united us in prayer for those men, all of us felt we were with them in a great fellowship of the spirit.

There is a small Christian church in Hirosake, Japan, which in its seventy-five years has produced over a hundred fulltime Christian workers. When on a cold afternoon in the autumn of 1951 I spoke to a group of workers gathered there, I was moved profoundly by the pastor's words as he told of the spiritual experiences which had come to him and his congregation in the hard days past. Strangely enough he did not dwell on their troubles but on their thankfulness for all the prayers which had been raised for them by their Christian brethren in other countries. He listed the gifts which had come from American churches as symbols of the unity of all Christians.

A little church was established in Clover Pass, Alaska. One of my friends told me of being there shortly after it was opened, when they were having a box social. The lady who played the piano happened to be his supper companion. It was obvious she had been drinking and she was embarrassed because he knew it. So she told him a little about her life and the emptiness of it in that little village, and then she said, "You know, doctor, no one ever seemed to give a damn for us until the church came." It is a sad day for the Christian church if it begins to think of itself as an institution to be served and supported instead of a fellowship of Christians with concern in their hearts for all men.

Some years ago in Pasadena, California, there was a young Negro boy who began getting into trouble with the law. He had grown bitter at the treatment his brother had received when he came back from the Olympic Games. He seemed to bear a grudge against everyone and he was developing a lawless attitude toward society. There was a young Methodist preacher in that town who was doing exceptionally fine work with boys. One day a judge called him and asked him if he would be willing to take responsibility for this boy who was getting into more trouble all the time, for if something was not done soon it would be too late. Karl Downs agreed to do what he could, and he spent a good deal of time with this one boy. His success was beyond even the judge's hopes and expectation. As a matter of fact, he became an outstanding representative of his race and a great athlete. You might be interested in knowing his name; it was Jackie Robinson. (If you do not know who he is, I shall say no more.)

Here is the work Christians are called upon to do. Here is the privilege which God gives to them. These things that really matter are not done by machinery, and they are not done through committees. As John Hall said many years ago, "Who feels the power of a tear in the eye of a committee?" All our organizing skill and all our efficiency can never be a substitute for the concern of the fellowship of the body of Christians called the Christian church. This good news has not been proclaimed loudly enough in our time. Some have foolishly assumed that it is no longer relevant, though just the opposite is the truth. For thousands of people in our society need to hear this good news of the concern of the church. It would restore a saving hope again.

4. FOR THE PREACHER

A disciple is not above his teacher, but every one when he is fully taught will be like his teacher. LUKE 6:40

I have always regarded the late Ernest Fremont Tittle as primarily a preacher. I suppose it is true that preaching was his great gift and the center of his largest influence. But when I was in his former parish for a few weeks some time ago, I learned that so far as many of his laymen are concerned, he will be remembered primarily as a pastor. One man told me that shortly before the famous preacher's death, he insisted on coming over to see him, though the layman offered to call on Dr. Tittle because of the minister's bad health. When he arrived, he said he had come to ask for help in finding a job for a member of the church in his late fifties who had unexpectedly lost his position. This was the kind of ministry which was not so well known outside the community, but it helps one understand why Dr. Tittle's preaching was heard gladly.

T. R. Glover was going home one night with a friend when he stopped suddenly and said emphatically, "I don't give tuppence for the man who goes into the pulpit to tell me what my duty is; but I give all I have to the man who tells me from whence my help cometh."[7] The man who tells another from whence his help comes speaks with authority when the man who hears him understands that he is an example of one who has obtained that help. For this kind of preaching is not telling people what their duty is but it is bearing witness to where strength can be found, and it is above everything else speaking out of the experience of one's own life.

[7] James, *op. cit.,* 110.

Our great temptation, of course, is to turn ourselves into professional spokesmen and manipulators. It is, in a word, to lose our sincere personal concern for every man. Sydney Franklin, the American bullfighter from Brooklyn, made a remark in his autobiography which is of some guidance to us here. One of his greatest teachers told him that because self-preservation is the strongest instinct, a man wants to seek cover when facing danger, and in bullfighting the cape is protection. But if you draw it to your body, as you would do instinctively, you are inviting disaster from the bull, so that the only safety is to move the cape away from oneself without a moment's hesitation.[8] And this is the temptation of the preacher. It is a temptation to cover ourselves with our professional robes and protect ourselves from the needs of the individuals whom we are called upon to serve.

There is a very interesting remark made in a modern novel.[9] A boy is talking about a play he had seen starring Alfred Lunt and Lynn Fontanne. He says they were very good but they were too good; they were supposed to be like people talking and interrupting each other. Then he makes the observation that if you do something too good, after a while you start showing off, and after that, of course, you are not good any more. I think I know what he is saying, for I have felt it when listening to some preachers. There is a smoothness and a perfection which seems to say that the role they have been playing through the years has now become so mechanical that they are no longer persons. The man who has not become professionalized is the man whose sincere concern makes him hesitate and grope from time to time. But that is much to be preferred over the smooth per-

[8] Franklin, *Bullfighter from Brooklyn,* Prentice-Hall, 1952, 14.
[9] Salinger, *op. cit.*

fectibility of the automaton or the professionalized expert. For when a preacher gets professionalized, it is worse than when it happens to any other man. The preacher who loses his tenderness and sympathy for all men not only does his job badly but he becomes a stumbling block for those who sincerely seek the Lord Jesus Christ. Richard Baxter described the real pastor's experience when he said, "I now see more good and more evil in all men than heretofore I did."[10]

Aldous Huxley said that Burton's *The Anatomy of Melancholy* is a mixture of dangerous nonsense and excellent sense, and then he adds, "Most of the nonsense derives from the current scientific theory; most of the sense from the open-minded empiricism of shrewd and kindly men who love their fellows."[11] It is possible for a man to know all the scientific theories of psychology and the workings of the human mind, and having lacked concern and compassion and love, work nothing but damage in his relationships with his brethren.

The prophetic function of the ministry must be rooted in concern. It is a sad day when a man excuses his bitterness by labeling it prophecy. But the preacher who has the shepherd's heart will be a foe to fear when the flock is in jeopardy. When Joseph Pulitzer announced his retirement in 1907, he issued a statement to the *World* and it is carried yet on the St. Louis *Post-Dispatch* masthead. He said he was confident

> That it will always fight for progress and reform, never tolerate injustice or corruption, always fight demagogues of all parties, never belong to any party, always oppose privileged

[10] *Autobiography,* Dutton, 1931, 115.
[11] Huxley, *op. cit.,* 168.

classes and public plunderers, never lack sympathy with the poor, always remain devoted to the public welfare, never be satisfied with merely printing news, always be drastically independent, never be afraid to attack wrong, whether by predatory plutocracy or predatory poverty.

You will search a long time to find a better description of what a man's ministry will be, if it holds a Christlike concern at the center.

Archibald Rutledge tells about the widow of a Negro preacher who was always looking after the poor and taking care of the orphans and illegitimate children in the community. He so appreciated her work that he built her a little home in his own back yard and equipped it with new furniture. But to his horror, the first thing she did was to invite into her home the most disreputable Negro woman in the county. "How could you have invited that creature into your pretty new home?" he asked. Her soft answer came back: "Jesus would."[12] That is the only answer that is any good. That is the final rule for our guidance. That is the ultimate and essential test of all Christian theology.

Not only in our personal life, but in our work we can lose our concern. There is a story about a sailor who had just come ashore and was most anxious to see his fiancée. He decided to send her a telegram, and so he went into the office, sat down, and pondered long and hard. Finally he came up with this message, "I love you. I love you. I love you." The girl at the desk said, "That is only nine words and you can send ten words for the same price." So he went back to the desk and struggled further. Finally he handed in this amended message, "I love you. I love you. I love you. Regards." I think sometimes a man may feel that way

[12] Day, *op. cit.*, 132.

about his pastor whom he hears proclaim from the pulpit his love for all men, but when face to face with human need he throws out a hasty "regards" and is on his way somewhere else. This is tragic anticlimax to our preaching. It is our temptation to use people for what we call high purposes but nearly always our own professional future is mixed up in it. It is still a sin if we seek to manipulate individuals for the sake of the organization rather than understand that the organization exists for the purpose of service to people. We ought to ask ourselves from time to time whether or not we are doing anything for men who cannot possibly help us. Are we as interested in serving the individual who cannot become the chairman of the finance committee or the president of the board? May we never give people the idea that we are looking at them as if we wished they were someone else.

One of my friends remarked not long ago that listening to some preaching was like watching wrestling on television. You never could make him believe, he insisted, that it is a real contest. It is a trick and a show but not actually a sport. Too many preachers, he thought, who are supposed to wrestle with the world, the flesh, and the devil have learned to put on a good act, but it is not real. And the thing which makes the difference between hypocrisy and reality is whether or not our concern for men caught in the wiles of the devil is sincere.

It it love in our hearts which makes us understand truth and gives us knowledge of right procedures in dealings with men. Nothing can take the place of the realism which comes to men who, out of the affection of lives devoted to the high calling of representing their Lord among men, ask no other reward than to interpret his will, mediate his presence, and proclaim his promises. We need the concern and earnestness of President Finney who, after pouring out his soul for the conversion of a list of people, added this rather unconventional phrase, "And Thou knowest, O Lord, that in these matters I am not accustomed to being denied." When with that faith and that persistence we pray and work for those to whom God has given us responsibility, our own lives will be good news of concern.

The grandson of Ernest Renan, who was also a skeptic, stopped at a rectory one day, and knocked. When the priest answered the door, the young man said, "Come out, I want to talk to you about a problem." But the priest replied, "No, you come in, I want to talk to you about your sins." Underneath the problems of life there is sin, and if we have learned to look at men through the eyes of Jesus, we shall not be misled into healing surface cuts when we ought to be dealing with diseases of the soul. Perhaps in no other part of our message does so much depend upon our personal lives. We cannot preach concern unless we are incarnations of it. Much will be forgiven us, much good will be done, and much love bestowed upon us if men hear this good news proclaimed in every relationship we have with them.

V *Good News of Eternity*

> The light shines in the darkness, and the darkness has not overcome it. JOHN 1:5

The more mature we become in the Christian life, the less disturbed we are with the critical problems involved in the obvious differences between the first three Gospels and the Fourth. That is, this New Testament phenomenon, which has caused so much bitter controversy through the years, remains a matter of scholarly curiosity, but it no longer appears as a threat to faith. We will go on trying to understand the essential nature of the Fourth Gospel, but our primary reaction is a great thanksgiving for the spiritual comfort and insight which have come to our fathers and to us from this latest of the New Testament's four portraits of our Lord.

A young friend of mine, who has been teaching Bible in church colleges, asked me to read a manuscript he had written on the Gospel of John. I hope that either it has been published or will be published in the future, for it has a number of very helpful observations regarding the nature of John's book. He says that we can think of the first three

Gospels as reporters bringing to us news concerning the actions and teachings of Jesus, while the Fourth Gospel is more like the editorial page of the paper, commenting on deeper and wider significance of the news. To a large extent it consists of a series of dialogues between Jesus and the spiritually dull, in which he seeks to help men see beyond the event to its significance from an eternal perspective. It is the opening up of the essential things of the Spirit to men who have grown blind and deaf to anything beyond their senses. And while this Gospel does not have the external movement of Mark, it is packed full of inner action. It does not take very much experience to teach us that the struggles of the soul are more terrifying and crucial than any outward conflict. The final purpose of the Fourth Gospel is not contemplation but decision.

John has more of a theological and doctrinal purpose than the other Gospels, although that is not entirely lacking in any of them. It should be said, however, that even from a historical point of view, John is given a more favorable position by critical scholars today than was the case fifty years ago. But this Book tries to give us not only a story about a teacher but it tries to make clear that he was divine and eternal. Here is portrayed One who was not merely immortal but One who conquered death by rising from the dead. The Resurrection is an act of God, and not just an inherent characteristic of the human soul. It is not so much an illustration of a doctrine of rewards and punishments to be experienced after death, as a mighty proclamation of eternal love that breaks into human experience destroying its pettiness and selfishness. So you will hardly ever pick up a Bible in a secondhand bookstore without finding that this

Gospel has been thumbed through more than any other book.

Arriving at some definite conclusions concerning the place where Jesus' words leave off and John's interpretation begins, becomes less and less significant. We find ourselves saying that this is what he meant to one spiritual genius toward the end of the first century, and this is what he has meant to his followers through the years. We thank God for the author of the Gospel, not so much for the facts he has given us concerning Jesus, as for his convincing assurance of the living Christ's eternal light which shines on those who know him.

1. REVELATION

And the Word became flesh and dwelt among us, full of grace and truth. . . . JOHN 1:14

Revelation is not confined to the New Testament nor is it an exclusive doctrine of the Fourth Gospel. But John has set forth in classic language the philosophy of Revelation and gives a Christian climax and fulfillment. When he says that the Word became flesh, he is placing Jesus in a cosmic setting and he is making clear that this is God's revelation of Himself. It is important to note that revelation comes from God and reaches us through a divine initiative. If we lose sight of this, or even minimize it in the least, then we are in great danger of becoming tritheists and of making the doctrine of the Trinity a stumbling block for all who have a real sense of the oneness of God. Perhaps in no other place does Christian orthodoxy need to re-examine its doctrines more than at this particular point. The main reason that Christianity has had no particular success in its mission to the Jews has been because a people with a fierce loyalty to the one God are sometimes scandalized by what sounds like a belief in two minor Gods. We need to keep it very clear in our own mind and in our preaching that the Word is the creation of God and that He made it become flesh. And Jesus is the revelation of God because God gave him the Spirit beyond measure.

In our time an extreme liberalism has denied the truth of the divine initiative of revelation. When I was in seminary some years ago, Christianity was regarded by many scholars as primarily a man's effort to understand a God who waited passively for the discovery. Because the human part of religion had been neglected, we swung to the other extreme and made the human part the whole. The Kingdom was regarded as something to be built by men, and salvation was only the practice of right ethics. Confidently we looked toward the brave new world of the future in which the new heaven and the new earth would appear when society had redeemed itself by curbing its evil tendencies, and educating itself into virtue.

Hugh Redwood said, "Preachers put forward their theories and elaborate their codes, but they rarely speak of personal experiment. They rarely tell you that they know of God's power to break a man of bad habits, because he has broken bad habits for them. And that is the very thing people would be interested to know."[1] John appeals constantly to the evidence of the witness, from the prologue to the end. While it is a wearisome matter to hear a preacher talk too much about himself and his family, it may be true that we have gone too far the other direction and failed to bear witness to what God has done for us. At any rate, let

[1] Menzies, *Fight the Good Fight,* Abingdon, 1949, 123.

this be my excuse to speak of my own experience in the hope that it may shed some light on another man's path.

I think the first year of my ministry, after finishing seminary, was one of the most unhappy and distressing times of my life. Having been trained to accept emphasis on human effort as being the chief thing in religion, I discovered that my human effort at least was not nearly enough. Things did not go too well and the congregation did not grow. It became more and more a matter of wondering whether some other profession might be more to my liking, and a real question haunted my mind as to whether the ministry was meant for me. It became increasingly apparent that I could not possibly go on, feeling the way I did, and if God wanted me to be His minister, He must give me an assurance and a confidence which was lacking. Looking back now, it seems that there came to me with the suddenness of a conversion the conviction that if it was God's work, then He had some responsibility for it; if He had called me to the ministry, He must surely want people to hear me preach. I began to read the promises God made through His prophets and especially through Jesus Christ, and finally grace enough was given to rest back upon faith in His power. It came to me that religion was not so much a matter of seeking God as it was an experience of being found by God, and that He had chosen even me and promised to hold me up.

One of the most astounding things about this revelation is that it is a living experience which continues to grow. For God has revealed himself through Jesus Christ who talks with us even now and in whose presence we are discovering constantly new visions of reality and new resources of confidence. It becomes clearer with every passing year that

Jesus Christ is the essential clue in this plot of life. Everything leads to him ultimately, because everything leads to God and he is the revelation of the Father. The good news of revelation is the good news of God's unfailing and persistent seeking of men.

William Cowper, a sensitive poet and fine Christian who wrote some of our greatest hymns, had long periods of utter depression and mental darkness when he thought he must have committed the unforgivable sin. John Newton tells about trying to bring his friend out of those terrible experiences but of his inability to offer any permanent healing. Cowper died finally with his reason in eclipse, but his friends declared that at the last there came over his face "a holy surprise." So when that vision comes of God's love for us while we were yet sinners, and his searching finds us even while we flee from Him, there comes into our lives a holy surprise which breaks down our anxiety and makes clear to us the source of our security.

But if this revelation comes from God, it certainly comes to men and usually it comes through men. This is at once the glory and terrible responsibility of the preacher, since men must assume that in him the spirit of God dwells and through him they will receive light and life. Amos could learn about God through a roaring lion and a basket of fruit. Hosea found Him in an unfaithful wife and a broken home. Isaiah could hear Him marching with the armies of Assyria, while Jeremiah heard Him speak through the work of a potter. But other men have had such experiences and heard no voice and felt no presence. When the voice spoke to Jesus in Jerusalem, some said it thundered (John 12:29). There is no mechanical, automatic process in God's revelation, and it must always wait until there is one who is able to understand and interpret.

The Christian preacher has learned that in Jesus Christ there is a final and complete revelation of God which he can proclaim with assurance. Here is all the truth a man needs to know, and here is all the guidance men need for the achieving of their best selves. In all the confusion of understanding ourselves and trying to determine what our destiny is, we have the life of our Lord and the wonderful word of the Resurrection. This is truly the good news of eternity, and when we lose it everything goes wrong with us. It is terrifying to note what happens to men when they try to live within the confines of this earth alone. "What's time?" asks Robert Browning, "Man has forever." For some strange reason, anything less than "forever" is not enough.

Henry Sloane Coffin has said that every man needs two things—a home and a horizon. It is a good and true word concerning our nature and our needs. We need a basic security and the assurance that we can rest in God who has been our help in all the ages past and is now and evermore will be our eternal home. We need also the far horizons lest we die of spiritual claustrophobia. The various ways of life we choose always promise one or the other of these values, but can hardly ever give us both. We preach the word of God who revealed Himself in a man, but who showed us also that we have eternal destiny and are of more consequence than the stars.

2. ETERNAL LIFE IN THE COMMONPLACE

And this is eternal life, that they know thee the only true God, and Jesus Christ whom thou hast sent. JOHN 17:3

The modern pulpit whenever it speaks of immortality

has a tendency to treat it as if it were a curious interest hovering about on the edge of life but of no immediate concern. Christian preaching ought to make of immortality a crashing crisis and a searching judgment on life's meaning. When the Fourth Gospel talks about eternal life, it talks about something that transforms the present and describes a luminous experience shedding a new glory upon every commonplace event. It makes a new heaven and a new earth even now and establishes our citizenship in heaven. It is not so much that we are urged to live for eternity, as a description of a kind of life that lives in eternity now.

The Fourth Gospel knows nothing about two distinct orders of time. It does not say that we live our life here under certain limitations, but one day after we die we shall enter into a new realm and be completely free from the limitations of this world. It seems to describe something that overlaps, something that interpenetrates, and something which brings heaven into earthly experience. This has not yet captured our contemporary Christian thought, and so far as most of us are concerned, dualism colors our thinking and our living. Some things are sacred, we assume, and some things are secular; some creatures are mortal and some are eternal. But the good news of the Gospel is of a mighty act of God which broke down barriers between this world and the next, as well as introducing into human life a foretaste of immortality. Now and again we find a man who has this ineffable quality and he brings a kind of light into every dark situation. His very conversation has the undertones of an everlasting experience, and he does his ordinary tasks with the quiet dignity of a priest serving at the altar. The good minister of Jesus Christ is one who not only has the accents of eternity in the pulpit but has an eternal quality in the commonplace relationships with his people. Perhaps the latter is the more significant in so far as preaching the good news of eternity is concerned. Such a quality of behavior seems to be a searching judgment on our own trivialities and the creation of a profound desire to establish our living within the larger framework.

In 1951, while on a trip around the world, I had the privilege of visiting Israel. I remember reading about a church that sent its minister to Palestine and then regretted it for the next twenty years. I have tried to refrain, therefore, from speaking very much about experiences which meant very much to me personally, but may bore others who have had neither the same experience nor the same interest. It is impossible to describe how a man feels when he walks where Jesus walked and looks out across a countryside that has known his presence. I was fortunate in having a guide who knew his Bible, and hardly an hour of any day passed that he did not point out the site where some Old Testament battle had been fought or the place where some Biblical incident happened. It was a week of almost constant stimulation and excitement, and my regret was that I had not found a way to visit this land before going to seminary and entering into a serious study of the Bible.

In the little town of Nazareth I did not find my chief inspiration at the holy places where the churches have been built, but in walking up a narrow little street full of open shops which have not been changed very much in the last nineteen centuries. They were preparing for a wedding in one courtyard and allowed us to come in if we promised to take no pictures. We watched them rehearse their dances which were to honor the bride and groom. I saw the moon on Galilee and climbed the Mount of Transfiguration at the close of the day. One day permission was given me to climb to the top of the old French monastery on the boundary line between the Jewish and Arab sections of Jerusalem. No more than a hundred feet away an Arab sentry eyed me with suspicion and distrust, and it came to me that even in Jesus' day the soldiers had been one of the noticeable features of the city's life, for it was not a free land. From the top of a shell-scarred co-operative building I looked across the valley to Bethlehem. I realized that the land where he lived and did his work was in some ways an ordinary country, not very fertile, with burned-out hills. It was full of cities with teeming populations of rich and poor and too many children with sore eyes. But the whole experience was summed up for me one day in this rather commonplace incident.

We had gone to Cana, where John says the miracle of turning the water into wine at the wedding feast took place. We started up the street and almost immediately we were surrounded by twelve to fifteen youngsters ranging in age from three or four up to ten or eleven. They were unkempt and dirty, and one or two of the larger girls carried infants on their backs. I asked my wife how old one of the little boys was and she said he must be about six, though I had difficulty in believing that he could have gotten that dirty in only six years. We came to the church, which has been erected on the alleged site of the wedding miracle, and went into the courtyard. We rang a bell to call the priest, and as we waited the youngsters stood around. Then suddenly the priest came storming out the door, and the children, for whom this was forbidden territory apparently, scattered as fast as they could before his anger. One little boy found it impossible to reach the gate and so he crouched down and hid behind a fountain until the priest had gone out into the street to chase the youngsters farther away. Then he dashed out in the other direction and escaped. Suddenly it came to me that these were the kind of children Jesus was talking about when he said, "Let the children come to me." I had always thought of them as the perfumed and bedecked infants we baptize at the altars of our churches on Palm Sunday. But they were nothing of the kind and his unforgettable graciousness and kindness to childhood was offered to street urchins. His words of compassion and love were not spoken in some special holy place, but by the sea, to the dirty, sweating people with neither culture nor wealth to make them comely. The eternity which shines through the Fourth Gospel is an eternity which manifested itself in the commonplace villages and streets of a commonplace country. What a wonderful thing it is if we can see this in our imagination and make it clear to every person, that God breaks into every human life and every human situation, with the beauty of His presence and the shining light of His countenance.

Our good news of eternity is the good news of a quality of life which is offered to every man now. It begins at the moment one comes into the presence of Jesus Christ and accepts him as the way. It redeems us from the monotony of our daily experiences and fills us with great expectation every moment. It came into a pagan world that had no confidence in the future and no belief in progress. The spirit of that world was summed up very well by Marcus Aurelius when he said, "The rational soul . . . realizes that our children will see nothing new, just as our fathers saw nothing different; so that in a sense the man of forty years of age, if he has any sense at all, has, in view of this sameness of things, seen all that has been or ever shall be." [2] This is a description of life with no divinity in it and no eternal note being sounded.

When you turn to the New Testament, however, you are amazed at the emphasis on the new and exciting things which have happened because Jesus came to dwell with men. There is talk about the new creature in Christ. Remember Paul's word: "Therefore, if any one is in Christ, he is a new creation; the old has passed away, behold, the new has come" (II Corinthians 5:17). Says Jesus to his followers, "A new commandment I give to you, that you love one another" (John 13:34). Or there is his word to Nicodemus, "Truly, truly, I say to you, unless one is born anew, he cannot see the kingdom of God" (John 3:3). Through it all there is the Gospel's insistence that something new has come into human life which puts it in a new perspective and gives it a new direction. This quality is nothing less than a revelation that every commonplace affair may receive the light of eternity and the ordinary life may have within it the shining glory of the presence of God.

One of Japan's great Christian leaders, Mrs. Tamaki Uemura, was the daughter of a Christian pastor who received so little financial support for his work that his family always lived in poverty. She says that when she was a little girl at school some of her companions found it amusing to ask her what she was going to wear at the next concert, and she always had to answer that she would wear whatever her mother had ready for her. Then they would laugh and say, "Oh, the same old stuffy thing you had on last time." Then one day she went home crushed and with a heavy heart to tell her mother what the girls had said. Her mother took

[2] Quoted by Baillie, *The Belief in Progress,* Scribner, 1951, 48.

her to her father's book cases and said, "Daughter, do you know that the dresses you cannot have to wear turn into these books? Father is a great minister of Christ. In order that he may preach the word of God without mistakes, he and I buy these commentaries. By wearing what we can afford to provide, you are helping him and me, and consequently you are serving Christ! You are truly very rich, are you not? Much richer than those people who have beautiful clothes!" Then she read from the Bible and the little girl felt that it was an honor and a privilege to give up a new dress to provide books for her father who was a minister of Jesus Christ.[3]

What a difference to all our life this eternal quality makes. Suddenly we discover that we find joy in what might otherwise have brought us dissatisfaction. That which seemed important is no longer very significant, and that which seemed secondary now looms as one of the most crucial of events. But above everything else this is the experience which enlightens all our living, so that even the common things of life shine with God's presence and meaning. If it is true that men can be told of an experience which will bring all eternity breaking in upon their everyday lives, this is good news indeed. It will rescue us from merely enduring the present in order to enjoy some great reward in the future. It enables every man to practice the presence of God and to live as eternal creatures every day.

When Roger Baldwin was up for reappointment as probation officer in St. Louis some years ago, a city official objected because he had heard Baldwin had leanings toward anarchism. But a local politician said that he was only flirting with the anarchist philosophy, but in no sense was he

[3] Leber, *op. cit.,* 209.

working at it. "It's just a sideline, like a man's religion," he explained. That satisfied the city fathers. And while all religion has been treated too much as a sideline in our time, we have been especially guilty of regarding eternity as of philosophical interest only. It has been a horrible blunder and our lives have grown dark because of it. This generation needs to hear that in Jesus Christ eternity dawned in men's hearts. Our overspecialization in the things of this world has produced narrow men. It is time to proclaim our whole Christian experience which includes this world and the next.

3. THE DIVINE DWELLS IN THE HUMAN

Abide in me, and I in you. JOHN 15:4

There has been considerable debate as to why John did not mention the virgin birth story. Whatever the reason may have been, his experience of the abiding reality of Jesus even after he had disappeared from human sight makes it clear that he did not conceive any impenetrable barrier between the human and the divine. This wonderful experience of the abiding presence of our Lord in the Christian's life finds its great emphasis and description in the Fourth Gospel. If the Word could become flesh, then divinity could dwell in the human, and the clear-cut distinction between body and soul, oftentimes associated with Greek thought, finds no agreement in the Christian's experience of unity with the risen Christ. This is not only the good news that God speaks to men but it is the wonderful assurance that God dwells with men.

It is this spiritual reality that penetrates every human experience and relationship. It is not physical ancestry that is important but spiritual kinship. The Jews boasted to Jesus,

"Abraham is our father." But the Master's reply makes clear that the facts of genealogy are not too important. "If you were Abraham's children," he replied, "you would do what Abraham did." (8:39)

Whenever we begin to think of divinity in its relationship to humanity, we are always forced to say something about the person of Jesus. This has been one of the central points of all Christian theology and it has caused as much debate as any single issue. What shall we say about Jesus Christ and how shall we describe his nature? This is not the subject of mere academic theological interest but it is a very practical question which each man has to face if he has been confronted by the claims of Christ. He must decide now whether or not he will become his follower and disciple. The preacher cannot ignore this question, if he would. It has been a source of some surprise to me to note how many people, including college students, are anxious for a man to speak some word about the nature of Jesus Christ. Above all other figures who ever appeared on this earth, Jesus has troubled men more with the mystery of who he was.

There are some who think they can be very exact and dogmatic about this matter. The fundamentalist preacher has no hesitation in telling his people exactly what they must think about Jesus and the exact language in which they must put their thoughts. It has been the attempt of theologians through the years to state with some preciseness what the essential nature of Jesus was, and we have been given formulas to express his relationship to God as well as the character of his humanity. It has been the attempt of the Christian church through the centuries to find some common definition of the being of Jesus that would unite all Christians.

The World Council of Churches has reached a formula which seems to be satisfactory to the vast majority of Protestantism. Its statement is that we must think of Jesus as God. I am glad that so many Christians have come together in a great unity and I would not for one moment make it more difficult by raising stumbling blocks for this unity. I shall continue to urge further co-operation by my own denomination in this Council rather than less, but I am frank to confess that the statement does not please me and it seems far from satisfactory. I would much prefer to have it say that God was in Christ, for I believe the testimony of the New Testament taken as a whole is against the doctrine of the deity of Jesus, although I think it bears overwhelming witness to the divinity of Jesus. I think it is time that we faced the truth that Christians are not going to get together in terms of precise formulations of theological propositions and that the World Council had better put more stress on common practice rather than common creedal statements.

Now if someone insists that the divinity of Jesus must be defined exactly, I would have to confess that I cannot do it for myself and it does not seem to me to be possible for others to do it. After all, what is divinity? Is it humanity at its best? Is it the state of being free from sin? How can the divine and the human mix in one person? Where does one begin and the other leave off? What was the status of our Lord before he was born in Bethlehem? Was his divine nature with him from the beginning, or is it something which was achieved? All these and a hundred other questions could be asked and I do not think they can be answered with any exactness.

I know in my own heart that Jesus Christ was unique and has within him qualities which are found in no other person. It is never enough to say that he was merely a good man who set a fine example, because there have been other good men who set fine examples but they never could do for their brethren what Jesus Christ does for us. He was a man and he was more than a man, yet he insists that every man could become even as he was. He was the Redeemer and the Saviour of mankind and of my life, but he lived among men in such a way that some of them could see nothing of the miraculous in him, and when the crucial decision had to be made, he was rejected.

Who can ever describe Jesus in words that will be satisfactory to others? Must we be too exact and too insistent that our definitions are final? A man stands on the shore of the sea on a hazy day and looks out across the horizon to where the sky and the sea meet, but to save his life he cannot tell where one begins and the other ends. Something of that same experience comes to us when we look at our Lord. He is a man, it is true, but somehow that humanity of his moves into divinity until we bow our heads and confess we are in the presence of the living God. The essential thing is that through Jesus we know that the divine comes into men's lives and that what happened so perfectly in him may happen, partially at least, in our own lives.

G. K. Chesterton wrote:

> There was a man who dwelt in the East centuries ago,
> And now I cannot look at a sheep or a sparrow,
> A lily or a cornfield, a raven or a sunset,
> A vineyard or a mountain, without thinking of Him;
> If this be not to be divine, what is it? [4]

What preachers need to do is to get more emphasis on the

[4] Used by permission of Miss D. E. Collins.

wonder of the experience and the miracle of our Lord's being, without entering into the kind of controversy which does not enlighten but only embitters.

One of the acute observers of our time said:

> In our century and almost within my memory covering some sixty-five years of awareness, the belief in the after-life has waned everywhere but chiefly among proletarianized city-dwellers. Is there a connection between a waning among these classes with a belief in an after-life, with its rewards and punishments, the loss of their sense of individuality, which they so readily abandoned to identify themselves with the only individuals that count, the Pharaohs of our day? [5]

Or, to put this in another way, is it true that when men lose some sense of the divine possibilities within them and the presence of divinity around them, that then they sink back more and more into the animal realm? We know too little about the nature of man and we can hardly find a definition which satisfies more than ourselves. But somewhere in the realm of religion there is that clue which cuts off mankind from the animal kingdom. It is a matter of divinity penetrating the human. It is the secret of our mystery and we shall never understand ourselves until we have some comprehension of this truth.

It is this good news which is desperately needed in our time to rescue us from disillusionment and despair. The emptiness of the generation has been brought about by men who revolted against the divine and became champions of the merely brutal. It has been a strange thing to observe how so many have assumed that if they could sink lower in the scale they would enter into their heart's desire. It is for the religious spokesman to insist that because the

[5] Berenson, *Rumor and Reflections,* Simon & Shuster, 1952, 34.

divine has touched us we can never be happy nor content unless we move up and not down. What a great thing it is if we can proclaim through our own experience in Jesus Christ that the hunger for divinity which is within us can be satisfied supremely by the presence of the Galilean. Preaching ought to have within it the wonderful announcement of John Monsell's hymn:

> Light of the world, illumine
> This darkened earth of Thine,
> Till everything that's human
> Be filled with the divine;
> Till every tongue and nation,
> From sin's dominion free,
> Rise in the new creation
> Which springs from love to Thee."

It is this good news of the divine life which has come to lighten every man that John teaches us to proclaim.

Many a visitor to Southern California finds his way to Forest Lawn Cemetery. There are not many places where a cemetery has become a center of beauty and great art. No one can visit that place without being impressed with the imagination of those who through the years have created replicas of famous churches and collected both copies and original masterpieces of art. Some time ago the director arranged for me to be given a special tour with a young man who knew the story of the growth of Forest Lawn. It came to me that few men would think that a cemetery offered very much possibility for a great creative career. But out of something which usually has to do with only the dead, here is something so alive and vital and vibrant that one thinks not so much of that which is dead but of that which is eternally alive. And there are men who go into churches which are supposed to be filled with all the vitality of the living Christ, and by their lack of imagination and a prosaic dullness which envelops everything, they turn the living Church of Christ into something dead. The good news which has to reach us first and then through us our brethren, is that the divine dwells in the human and that there is no human task which cannot glow with the implications of eternity. It is a part of our message that the one who made a poor, burned-out country into a "Holy Land" can set our burned-out lives aglow with his shining presence.

4. FOR THE PREACHER

I have said this to you, that in me you may have peace. In the world you have tribulation; but be of good cheer, I have overcome the world. JOHN 16:33

One of the besetting sins of modern preachers is to be content with little themes instead of remembering that we are to proclaim the good news of eternity. We paint on too small a canvas and we are content to bring some small comfort for some particular human worry rather than bring our whole life into the light of eternity. If topical preaching has captured the market in America, as I believe it has, then our topics have become too small and our accent is too much on our culture or on sentiment or on mere temporary considerations. We talk too much about the questions that occupy the periodicals and fill up the newspapers. Too much preaching is in the realm of commentary but very seldom in the realm of revelation.

In this of course we are the products of our time and we have yielded to the disease of our generation. Any man who reads modern novels knows how seldom he finds one that is big enough to stretch his mind or sound a new note in depth. As a matter of fact, some of our novelists make no pretense to do anything but deal with small themes and think they have fulfilled their function if they deal with them smoothly and artistically. I do not plead now for books which drive home some particular moral, nor would I insist that novelists ought to write only within the general framework of the Christian faith. But it does seem to me that when men can no longer wrestle with questions that are important, or at least reveal that there has been some struggle within them to face ultimate issues, they need not be surprised if their work is considered trash.

When Sinclair Lewis received the Nobel Prize for Literature in 1930, he took the occasion to speak his mind concerning some neglected writers, among whom he mentioned Eugene O'Neill. He said:

> And had you chosen Mr. Eugene O'Neill, who has done nothing much in American drama save to transform it utterly, in ten or twelve years, from a false world of neat and competent trickery to a world of splendor and fear and greatness, you would have been reminded that he has done something far worse than scoffing—he has seen life as not to be neatly arranged in the study of a scholar but as a terrifying, magnificent, and often quite horrible thing akin to the tornado, the earthquake, the devastating fire.

May God send us men who can perform a similar service for the modern pulpit!

A great deal is made today of the sickness of the legitimate stage. Everything is blamed, from television to the lack of faith in this generation. But one thing seems to be overlooked, curiously enough, and that is that most plays are not worth seeing. It is their utter triviality that is boring, for they have no real comedy within them and no characters mature enough to make the difference between cheap vulgarity and drama. This is not the judgment of a moralist but the protest of one who thinks that $4.40 is too much to spend for the privilege of being bored.

A friend of mine returned some time ago from a visit to Las Vegas and Boulder Dam. He was commenting on the glitter of Las Vegas and what a spectacular sight it was to see all the electric signs in action in this fabulous community dedicated to gambling and entertainment. He said that he noticed the difference between Las Vegas, and the great Boulder Dam with its clean lines and its spectacular engineering skill. Then another man spoke up and pointed out that the electrical power produced at Boulder Dam is sent down to Las Vegas to be used for the cheap purposes which had disgusted my friend. Maybe the lesson is that we are using great power for little purpose or, to put it in our homiletical framework, we are using the good news of eternity to illustrate little inconsequential themes.

A group of the nation's top entertainers were gathered one evening at the Friar's Club. They had been reminiscing about the good old days and their past experiences. Their recollections had made them tender and sentimental, when George Burns went over to the piano and began to play "There's No Business Like Show Business," which was sung with great gusto by the group. After they had finished singing, George Jessel stood up and said, "The show must go on. The show must always go on." In the silence that followed the old bromide, Groucho Marx brought a swift end to the emotion of the meeting by asking "Why?" The story says that they were so angry with him, they decided to take away his membership in the Club, but he heard about it and resigned before the action could take place. In his letter he said, "I refuse to belong to a Club that will accept me as a member."

In the midst of so many of the pretensions of our time, it is necessary for somebody to ask that simple question, "Why?" We do so many things, we think so many thoughts, and we go through so many motions which we have been told are expected. But if some clear, blunt question were asked suddenly, we might see the triviality and the stupidity of it all. It is the preacher's task very often to bring an eternal judgment to bear upon a contemporary attitude. How little some of our activities seem to be, when the good news of eternity breaks in upon them.

We are guilty too often of not only small themes but of temporary topics. H. G. Wells one time had a keen insight into the nature of his own work, especially his fiction, when he said that it was dead because it dealt with matters of only topical interest because he had written as a journalist. If a man can escape the temptation of using his old sermons to save him from the hard work of preparation each week, he ought to save some of them to see how they look to him after five years' time. This is usually one of the most disillusioning experiences any preacher can have, for he will discover that there are too many of his sermons which have no lasting relevance, and were of merely passing concern. Too much of our preaching is like yesterday's newspaper, of no further use except to line a shelf. "Life-centered Preaching" sometimes means that we deal with only those issues which interest people, and like newspaper headlines they are often relatively unimportant. Sometimes I have preached a New Year's sermon based on the newspaper files of ten years before, reminding the congregation of what seemed significant on that day. Nearly always one discovers that the real news was never noticed and that the happening which so agitated and excited the people was not half so important as they thought. Too much preaching is like this and we can hardly escape it unless we have a real sense that our good news is of eternity.

There are sermons of the great preachers of the nineteenth century which are as fresh today as they were when they were first delivered. It may be a prejudice on my part, but it seems to me that this was more characteristic of the preachers of the nineteenth century than it has been of the preachers of the twentieth century. If most of them lacked a proper number of illustrations and did not refer to so many contemporary events, they dealt with themes that will be true a thousand years from now. Because they were so often rooted in the Bible, their approach is fresh. Let a man ask himself how this sermon will sound in another ten years and whether or not it would have had a word for the people of the eighteenth century. We can be saved from much of our tendency toward triviality and littleness if we remember always that we are proclaiming the good news of eternity.

Let us preach the great, unchanging themes which can be read now and can be read years later. There has been such a turn toward religion on the part of intellectuals that even *The Parisian Review* commented on this trend in a series of articles. I do not know how others will interpret this trend, but to me it says that men need some word about eternity. We try to convince ourselves that the passing show is enough, and whatever years we have been granted here we will use, and then call it a day. But we have been so created that there is a hunger for immortality and we need to hear some clear word about the values which never change and the destiny that is forever. We can never escape entirely the truth that we are pilgrims here and that although we talk about mother earth, our home is somewhere else. It is for us to link up men's lives with their heavenly home.

When Erasmus was in Paris, he wrote to a friend: "As soon as I receive any money, I will buy Greek authors and afterwards some clothes." Because most people have been more concerned about clothes than with Greek authors, the modern pulpit too often has geared its message to clothing and not to the unseen values which never fade away or die. Said Robert Browning:

> 'Tis an awkward thing to play with souls,
> And matter enough to save one's own.[6]

We had better make sure that we have the values right in our own lives, so that when men hear us preach the good news they will hear the solemn and majestic tones of a life that knows no dying.

[6] "A Light Woman."

VI *Good News of Redemption*

> For I am not ashamed of the gospel: it is the power of God for salvation to every one who has faith. . . . ROMANS 1:16

The good news of salvation cannot be confined to any particular book in the New Testament, nor indeed can it be confined to the New Testament alone. There is a sense in which the whole Bible is the story of God's gracious desire to save men. There are other themes which run through the Book, it is true, but soon or late they all converge in the marvelous drama of God's saving action. We speak sometimes of Biblical heroes but indeed, as Henry Sloane Coffin has pointed out, the entire Biblical literature reflects but one hero and one chief actor, who is the living God.[1] The assumption of the Bible is that God is engaged primarily in bringing about the salvation of the world, and His processes of salvation are observable in history and are experienced in personal life.

Yet when one chooses a single person to represent the effective presentation of this good news of God's salvation

[1] Coffin, *op. cit.*, 2.

in Christ, the name "Paul" leaps so immediately and powerfully into the mind that one seeks no further. Biblical criticism has not always been kind to St. Paul, and there have been periods when scholars sought to discredit his significance. There have been other times when an attempt was made to show that he was a bad influence in our religion rather than a good one. But these unworthy periods pass and the great Apostle stands in clearer and purer light with every passing generation.

Paul is the supreme example of a man frustrated and defeated, who found salvation in an experience of Jesus Christ. Precisely because he was no ordinary man, he saw the profound implications of his experience and he described them in unforgettable language. Not every man will feel the same as Paul felt even when the same valid experience comes to him, and not every one of us will be able to probe the depths of its meaning as he did. But through all Christian history, it has been his insight and ability to analyze what was involved that has kept the Christian church on the main line. The central significance of Christianity as a religion of salvation is kept ever before us by the Pauline Epistles. It is not too much to say that whenever Christianity has been at its best, it has been roughly speaking the Christianity of St. Paul.

An ancient Greek story says that outside the city of Thebes there was a monster called the Sphinx and to every person who passed by, he gave this riddle: What creature walks in the morning upon four feet, at noon upon two, at evening upon three? Anyone who failed to answer the riddle was destroyed. But Oedipus finally solved it by answering that it is man who crawls on all four as a baby, then walks upright on two feet in maturity, and finally in old age moves with the aid of a staff. Professor Caird has suggested that our generation faces a similar riddle and if we cannot find the answer to it, we will be destroyed. But in our day man is not the answer to the riddle but is himself the riddle.[2]

Now every religious revival has been a renewed discovery of the shining truth, that in Christianity we have the solution to man's riddle. It is the answer, because it can save him from himself, and the preacher who has truly accepted this becomes, in his own parish at least, a minor incarnation of the Apostle. In John Wesley's Journal for May 20, 1742, he tells of overtaking a man on the road and engaging him in conversation concerning religion. Wesley suggested that they keep to the practical things lest they might grow angry with each other. He says:

> And so we did for two miles, until he caught me unawares and dragged me into the dispute before I knew where I was. He then grew warmer and warmer; told me I was rotten at heart, and supposed I was one of John Wesley's followers. I told him, "No, I am John Wesley himself." Upon which . . . he would gladly have run away outright. But, being the better mounted of the two, I kept close to his side, and endeavored to show him his heart, until we came into the street of Northampton.

It is that confidence and sheer persistence that explains part of the power of the Wesleyan movement. It is the lack of these things that explains the weakness of our present Christianity. Can we imagine what it would do to our preaching if we really believed that our message was the power of God to save all who accepted Christ in faith? Because the recovery of this assurance is so significant, we

[2] Caird, *op. cit.*, 1.

must try to understand the essential nature of the Christian experience of salvation.

1. GRACE

For you know the grace of our Lord Jesus Christ. . . . II CORINTHIANS 8:9

What does the New Testament mean when it speaks of the grace of God or the grace of the Lord Jesus Christ? Certainly there is a sense in which none but his loved ones can understand it. No one who has not experienced it will be able to enter into its meaning with any fullness. So we must try to explain what it means and we must try to put into plain words the meaning of this grace which we are to preach. Francis Greenwood Peabody said in his Beecher Lectures that there are three distinctive marks of the man who has been influenced by Jesus Christ. They are:

> Poise, simplicity, peace—all these mark the character which issues from the teachings of Jesus; and when his followers wished to sum up in a single phrase the most dominant aspect of this moral creation, and a special blessing which it received from him, they turned to one further word, which soon became the accepted form of benediction in his name. It was the word "grace." [3]

Perhaps this is the best we can do as we seek the definition. And yet even these words fall upon our ear as being not quite adequate to say all that is in our heart. The grace of God is His gift of life which is offered without price and which suddenly appears to be all that we have sought or desired. No man turns away from it once he really understands it, and there is nothing in any philosophy or any rival faith that can compete with the richness of its promise.

[3] Quoted by Jones, *op. cit.*, 195.

It is that golden extra of kindness and love and generosity which is offered by the living God to every person. No sensitive person expects it as his just due, but always he knows that it comes utterly undeserved.

In all these great truths of religion we must find human analogies which alone can set the door ajar so that we may enter into the deeper experience. I have a friend who constantly illustrates grace, to my mind. There are so many thoughtful things he does which never occur to me. A little gift or a note arrives at the most unexpected times, and they are always just the right gifts and just the right words. These are the experiences that lift up our hearts and tell us that in these personal relationships we have the real wealth of human experience. I think it must flow from the life that has more love in it than other lives and has been made wise and sympathetic by the nobility of almost complete unselfishness.

It is amazing how some little incident in the past can sometimes be remembered for so long and mean so much. A good many years ago when I was a schoolboy, I delivered morning newspapers. The financial condition of the family was such that if there was to be any spending money at all, I had to earn it. This seemed to be the only practical way to go about it, but it meant arising at 3:30 A.M., which was never easy, and was almost impossible if I had been out the night before and was particularly tired. I can remember a number of mornings when the alarm went off right in my ear and I did not hear it. One winter morning I managed to get up and ride down to the press room through a cold rain. There was a wind blowing and it seemed to blow right through my clothing into my body. Do you know how wet and miserable one can get on a bicycle on a rainy morning? After getting my papers, folding them and putting them in the bag, I finally managed courage enough to leave the warm room. I rode up the alley, and there parked at the corner was our old Ford. My father was in it waiting for me. He said, "Son, it is too cold and miserable for you to ride your bicycle on the route this morning. You put it over there in the corner and I will drive you." I can remember my feelings, as if this had happened yesterday. My father had to go to work early in the morning and I had no legitimate claim whatsoever upon him for this kindness. I think I came closer to him that morning and I had a more profound understanding of what fatherhood meant than at any other time in my life. Somehow when I am trying to define what the grace of God means, I think of that act of my own father who had gone far beyond a reasonable claim because of his love and concern. It is this kind of an experience of God's grace that redeems and cleanses us.

His grace comes to destroy our pride in our own goodness and in our own righteousness. He who has been the recipient of this grace no longer takes refuge in his own merit or his own moral superiority. When a man is able to bow his head and pray for mercy for himself and his brethren, it is an experience which brings humility and makes possible the right relationship with other persons and God. Out of that humility comes the freedom and the dignity of men who no longer pretend and no longer are proud. But most of all, this is an experience of joy and assurance because it tells us the eternal God is more forgiving than we ever imagined, and He is more concerned than we ever believed.

Sherwood Anderson, in many ways a frustrated and unhappy man, wrote to a friend in 1934:

> I want to write one joyous book before I die . . . not at all sentimentally joyous, but having in it a deeper joy. . . . Isn't there a deeper lesson God wants us to know, and that we, like perverse children—that's what we are, quite hopelessly children—that we will not know? [4]

What this man longed for, the Christian experiences, and what he vaguely felt was a possibility, we know.

In the eighteenth century, John Newton wrote some great hymns, and all of them were reflections on his own experience. He came from a good home and went to sea. He was impressed by the Royal Navy and was so bitter that he became a bad seaman and tried to escape. He was caught and punished and in a kind of wild rebellion turned to all manner of evil. He prided himself on being an atheist and ridiculed anything that was decent or religious. He found himself finally serving a slave trader in Africa and sank down to the depths of humiliation and despair. Finally he decided he must go to England again, and on the homeward voyage his ship was caught in a terrific storm so that it looked as if it would go down. Something happened to him at that moment and he knew if he was to be saved, God would have to save him. Somehow the ship came through. He went home, married a fine girl, and returned to the church. Finally, after great opposition and many difficulties, he was ordained a priest in the Church of England, and became an influential minister. But he never could forget his past life and what God had done for him, which he summed up in a hymn my mother used to sing and which is familiar to many Christians.

[4] Jones, *Letters of Sherwood Anderson,* Little, Brown, 1953, x.

Amazing grace! how sweet the sound,
That saved a wretch like me!
I once was lost, but now am found,
Was blind, but now I see.

The beginning of the experience of salvation is an awareness of this amazing grace of God in Christ which sought us and died for us while we were yet sinners.

2. FAITH

Therefore, since we are justified by faith, we have peace with God through our Lord Jesus Christ. ROMANS 5:1

Our life has become more complicated than at one time we thought was possible. Fundamental issues once seemed rather clear and we assumed that adoption of general principles should lead us to success. This meant of course that we could have confidence in knowledge and education, since our troubles sprang from ignorance and prejudice. But the issues, if they ever were simple, are certainly no longer so obvious. With all our knowledge, we are more aware now of the final limitations and incompleteness of all knowledge. Life evidently is much more than a human affair, and the mysteries of the future lie beyond the power of the human mind to control. It is not that we do not know enough facts, but it is the haunting suspicion that if we knew all the facts there are still elements decisive in human affairs which are beyond our power to manipulate.

Because Christianity has always understood this, it has recognized that men live by faith; which is to say, that men must recognize God's ultimate Lordship and their final dependence upon Him. We are saved finally when we accept by faith His grace and take it not as a sentimental and unessential coloring of our own wisdom, but as the foundation on which we have to build our lives and societies. Essentially our faith is the recognition that God will always have the final word, that we are destined to do His will, and through the doing of that will, come to the full realization of our human potentiality.

Jeremiah proclaimed it clearly in these words:

> Thus says the Lord: "Let not the wise man glory in his wisdom, let not the mighty man glory in his might, let not the rich man glory in his riches; but let him who glories glory in this, that he understands and knows me, that I am the Lord who practice kindness, justice, and righteousness in the earth; for in these things I delight, says the Lord." JEREMIAH 9:23–24

One of Israel's deep insights was the limitation of knowledge. A reading of the Old Testament reveals a very different spirit than is found in the philosophy of the Greeks or in the religion of China. The great teachers of Greece had supreme confidence in reason, so that the Greek mind would have had little sympathy with this word of Jeremiah. It would have seemed to the sophisticated philosophers the rude sentiment of an untrained ignorant backwoodsman. The Christian who reads the religious books of China is impressed with the great emphasis placed upon common sense and intellectual solutions. There is an assumption that a basic framework of thought can be discovered which will provide all that men and nations need to gain the good life. But Israel never could accept this, for she was suspicious of the wisdom of men and the cleverness of the human mind. There was in her thinking only one basic assurance for man, and that was the knowledge of God and the understanding of the Almighty's will.

But this discovery was open not only to the well-trained

and educated but to the most humble, as the birth stories of Jesus make so clear. Wise men came from the East bringing their gifts, but they laid them at the feet of a newborn baby with only a manger for his crib. The story is saying to us that all the wise men of the world shall finally bow humbly before a Galilean carpenter whose simple, perfect life reveals the final and essential truths about God and man. Let us remember that according to Luke it was only the shepherds, plain humble men, who heard the angels sing. So these very wonderful stories which have gathered around the birth of our Lord are luminous with faith and full of the insistence that reason must bow in humility, and that vision and understanding come to the unsophisticated.

A scientific age finds it difficult to understand the meaning of Paul's experience. He had received the knowledge and training his generation afforded. The transformation came when he lost his confidence in his knowledge and discovered his salvation through faith. It was not in himself that he found redemption, and it was not in reason that he was to discover the right path. In a wider and more significant sense, he discovered what the repentant Communist Whittaker Chambers experienced. In his autobiography, Chambers talks about breaking with communism and trying to escape back into the other world. He took a number of precautions to escape and then discovered that none of these precautions had really saved him. He writes, "How silly to suppose that any man by his own effort can ever save himself."[5] How foolish indeed to think that a man can save himself by his own wisdom or a generation can save itself by its own cleverness. Our salvation lies in accept-

[5] Chambers, *Witness,* Random House, 1952, 55.

ing God's grace for us through faith, for by faith we are saved and that not of ourselves.

Faith always involves the element of response. It always involves risk and the willingness to plunge over the abyss, as the neo-orthodox brethren like to emphasize. Finally, it is experiencing God's grace in such measure that one is willing to trust it far beyond the immediate experience. It is a willingness to go all the way on the assumption that His grace is universal and eternal. Men who say yes to God in Christ do not know all that is involved in that decision; they can never tell just where the road will lead or what will be demanded of them tomorrow. They know only that there has come to them enough light to live by now and they believe that that light will move ahead of them along the path. We will do no violence to the Christian experience if we paraphrase verse 105 of the 119th Psalm, and say, "Jesus Christ is a lamp to my feet and a light to my path." For it was the Christian experience that in the living presence of Jesus Christ that Word became flesh, and in his grace there is the illumination for the next step and light for all the years ahead.

John Newton was cured of the tendency to censure other people by an experience related by one of his friends who may have been the prison reform leader, John Howard. This man had gone to the prison to speak to a woman who was under sentence of transportation. He spoke to her of her crime and eternal punishment, but she seemed strangely indifferent. In spite of the fact that she stood in danger of hell and would be the first to admit it, she seemed to care very little. It was then that John Howard changed his approach and began to speak of the grace of God, of His love and redemption. At once the woman was interested, then affected, and finally comforted. This made a very great impression on John Newton and affected all his preaching.[6] It does not help too much to beat other people or ourselves over the head with hard words. Salvation begins when the grace of God penetrates unto our hearts and we find faith to accept that experience for ourselves and offer it to all men.

3. FREEDOM

For freedom Christ has set us free; stand fast therefore, and do not submit again to a yoke of slavery. GALATIANS 5:1

There is always the danger of Christians taking pride in being free from things they never were tempted to do. A woman in a prayer meeting one time testified that she was saved from tobacco, from drink, and from the theater. This was somewhat of a surprise to her pastor, and so he called on her the next day to say that he did not know that she smoked but he was so happy that she had been freed from that habit. "Oh," she replied, "I have never smoked in my life." Then the pastor suggested she must have been freed from the drink habit. She confessed that she had never touched a drop of it. Finally he said to her that he was pleased at least she had been set free from the evil influence of the theater, but then she confessed that she had never entered the theater. She had been rejoicing in being saved from sins that she had never really wanted to commit.[7] We would have to admit that if this is all the Gospel can do for us, it is not anything to get very excited about. There is in truth a narrow kind of freedom which some people proudly claim to possess which is only another kind of slavery.

[6] Martin, *John Newton,* Heinemann, 1950, 173.
[7] Marney, *These Things Remain,* Abingdon, 1953, 47.

Paul's experience of salvation was an experience of freedom, but it went to the very depths of his nature. He saw humanity as falling into one of two categories. First of all there was the natural man which he describes in his Letter to the Romans, and he assumes that it is the condition of every man until he has been saved by God. The natural man is not necessarily a depraved individual and he does not always choose evil deliberately. He may be a Pharisee who with all honesty is seeking to keep his life pure and moral. He may be a man with good intentions and decent impulses. But the natural man is the victim of a frustration which, if he is very sensitive, drives him to despair. The very rules he seeks to draw up to protect himself become the chains which enslave him. Finally the haunting suspicion takes hold of him that he can never completely trust himself. He finds himself doing the thing which he did not think was possible and he comes to the close of a day asking himself if the daily record reflects his true nature. It is spiritual and moral powerlessness which he sees finally as the real truth about himself. There are things which ought to be done and he understands his obligation to do them, but too often, when the test comes, he fails.

Paul found his answer in Christ when he became what he called a spiritual man. This was his salvation by faith and this was freedom. It was the discovery of a reservoir of power always available to him, and the realization that when he dared to confess his own unworthiness and weakness he could be free from the haunting fear of guilt. But it was not merely being free from guilt that impressed him the most. It was the amazing discovery that now God was able and willing to do for him what he never could do for himself. The pictures he uses to express this experience have seemed extreme to many a modern man. He talks about being dead and coming to life. But he uses one figure of speech which is plain enough to this generation—he had been a slave and he has been set free. It is release from the disillusionment and despair which moral failure and sin have created.

Rubinstein was in New York City over a weekend and he was asked if he would like to attend church. "Yes," he replied, "if you will take me to hear a preacher who will tempt me to do the impossible." The musician rightly understood that a religion that is not able to expand a man's vision of what a man can do, and make him dream great dreams, is futile. When a man has accepted the grace of God by faith, he is set free from all the ordinary limitations, and in place of his frustration and fear, he will testify, "If God be for us, who can be against us?" A religion that saves men is always a religion that sets men free. One of the sure signs of salvation in Christ according to St. Paul, is the experience of release.

Once Paul had experienced liberty, he became a great liberal spirit fighting for the right of Christianity to free itself from the unnecessary restrictions of the law. It is a pity that there are not more of our fundamentalist brethren who understand this. They quote Paul as if he would be in sympathy with their position; but if they understood him at all, they would see him as one opposed to any interpretation which set boundaries to the mind or sought to sum up the meaning of Christ within a dogma. It was precisely because Paul had been set free from the restrictions of law that he entered into the full experience of Christian salvation.

Any tendency to reduce religion to a creed is a bad tendency. For if it has its way and goes far enough, it takes all the life out of Christian experience and turns it into a barren, dry legalism. It was Castellio who said a good many years ago:

> My confidence in the authority of sacred authors is confirmed when I see them so intent upon the salvation of men as to be unconcerned for words. Their reliability is thereby manifest. Those who tell the truth do not strain at words. It is precisely liars who aim at a particular verbal consistency to hide their deception.[8]

While it would be going too far to say that the extreme literalist is always a liar, it is no exaggeration to say that he always misses the truth because he is satisfied with a part of it if he can keep it safe within the limitations of his own definitions. It is indeed a contradicton to hear men talk about salvation with a mean, small spirit that prefers the darkness of slavery to the light of freedom.

Paul could promise freedom and salvation with authority because he could also write the 13th chapter of I Corinthians. For it is love that sets men free and it is love that saves them. St. Francis de Sales said in 1612 that it was the division between the bishops, the Sorbonne, and the Orders which gave heresy its opportunity. He writes, "Whoever preaches with love, preaches efficiently against heresy, though he may never utter a controversial word."[9]

The controversy between the liberal and the conservative is always helpful to all if the spirit of both sides remains Christian. Theological debate sharpens perception if bitterness does not enter into it. But when religious experience narrows the soul and makes the spirit intolerant and hate-

[8] Quoted by Bainton, *The Travail of Religious Liberty*, Westminster, 1951, 117.

[9] *Oeuvres*, VI, 309.

ful, then whatever else may be said has happened to the man, it can never be said that he has been saved. One of the best signs of salvation is the free spirit and the free mind which are created by the free love of God in Christ.

Ecumenical movements never become relevant in the world if they do not comprehend that Christian unity is not to be obtained on the basis of a common creed. It is wasteful and futile to spend too much time in conferences trying to get delegates from different communions to agree on a precise definition of a Christian theological proposition. Creeds go wrong when they become more than general affirmations of truths common to all Christians. Whenever they try to become too precise, they automatically exclude vast numbers of sincere and honest Christians. Exact agreement is not possible between ministers of the same denomination, nor is it something one should wish to attain. Why are we concerned or troubled when men persist in defining their experiences differently and put their emphasis on the Christian revelation according to their own traditions? I am aware that I speak as a Methodist with Methodist emphasis when I say that the significant thing is a Christian experience and not a Christian definition. I feel so strongly, however, that Christian unity should be based upon a common practice rather than a common wording of our theological insights, that a vain attempt to heal the divisions of the church through words rather than through deeds seems to me a waste of time and a futile pastime for mature Christians.

It may seem like the height of presumption to suggest that in this field we have a great deal to learn from the military services. A preaching mission for the Air Force in Europe opened my eyes to some things which we have not truly appreciated. There is a sense in which the Ecumenical Church has arrived much more in the military services than it has in the communities of America or Europe. If it is true that God makes even the wrath of man to praise Him, perhaps this military necessity of the contemporary world is being used to bring about a truly ecumenical Christianity more than the conferences at Amsterdam or Evanston.

The military chaplain comes from a particular denomination, but he is first of all a member of a common fellowship of Christians. He is associated with men from other communions and he plans a common program and a common worship service for men of all communions. This does not mean that these men have suddenly forgotten their theological differences, as I well know, having spent more than one evening in theological discussions which generated considerable warmth. The Presbyterian or Episcopalian is still far removed from the Nazarene or the Southern Baptist in theological assumptions. But I have seen a real unity of spirit and activity which seems to me to be a preview of what the Ecumenical Church will be.

I preached one Sunday morning at the American chapel in Wiesbaden. After the service was over, I stood at the door to greet the people as they left the church, while another line of people passed on the other side of the doorway entering the church. By the time my congregation had gone out and I had taken my topcoat from the office, the Catholic priest was already at the altar and the Catholic congregation was kneeling while the organ played. One does not see this in civilian life. But if it ever becomes plain to us that in a sense we are soldiers united in a common crusade, then this new thing may happen to us and the Ecumenical Church will be among us. But it will be an

Ecumenical Church of free associations, and a great part of the saving experience we have in Christ will be the loosening of our fears and suspicions when our brethren say things differently and emphasize propositions we tend to neglect.

The extreme literalist's position in regard to the scriptures is carried to its logical conclusion by a Dutch Anabaptist who read of Isaiah's vision in the Temple and was sure that it was to be literally applied to him. So he took a live coal from off the hearth and touched his lips, but he did not say as did the Prophet, "Here am I; send me," because for two weeks he could not say anything.[10] Whatever the religious experience may be that makes men seek refuge in some legalism or some narrow, rigid theology, it is never a truly Christian experience. Christ came to set us free. The great Apostle to the Gentiles found in his own life a freedom which he talks about in his letters constantly. For when the grace of the Lord Jesus Christ is accepted by faith, then we are free indeed.

4. FOR THE PREACHER

Brethren, join in imitating me, and mark those who so live as you have an example in us. PHILIPPIANS 3:17

The preachers of salvation have to be men with sparkle in their talk and light on their faces. They are men who present no demand without a gift and they take time for diagnosis only because they have a cure. Usually, they speak at least ten words for the Saviour for every word of judgment. After we have agreed that the church services should be in order and have dignity, still when the Christian faith breaks in upon a congregation with real power, there

[10] Bainton, *op. cit.*, 128.

is always a sense of expectancy and spontaneity which no set ritual can ever quite contain. Bernard Berenson says that a diplomat in Rome once told him that whenever an important foreign personage was coming to the city, information had to be obtained as to the proper amount of enthusiasm with which he was to be received.[11] There are preachers who seem to imply by their delivery and their person that the one they are introducing is of such small significance that the least amount of enthusiasm is enough. If it comes to us that we are introducing the King to his subjects, there will be on our part a sense of the tremendous importance of what we do and our manner will say that we are engaged in something so wonderful that we can hardly find words to express this high honor. It was not only the eighteenth-century Deists who thought that enthusiasm was of the devil, but many a modern congregation has been led to believe by the kind of preaching it has listened to that the good news of salvation is a very heavy, painful, wearisome subject.

The time has come for a revival atmosphere to be created in the respectable churches of America. How marvelous it would be if men went to church on Sunday morning a little fearful of what might take place and quite uncertain as to what their frame of mind would be when they departed. The prayer which pleads for "a divine surprise" ought to be on our lips as we enter our pulpits and shake us loose from the deadly monotony of our little moralisms. Said the late Archbishop of Canterbury in his great book, *Nature, Man and God:*

> Thus it could come about that David Hume should compose his Dialogues on Natural Religion, so cogent an argumentation,

[11] Berenson, *op. cit.,* 97.

so urbane, so devastatingly polite, in a moment when John Wesley was altering the characters of thousands in the course of English History by preaching salvation through the precious Blood—a theme which one suspects that Hume and his friends would have thought ill-suited for refined conversation.[12]

We read our prayers and they are literary masterpieces. The choir sings an anthem that is musically correct, and our sermons are intelligent but irrelevant. Then we wonder what is the secret of the uncultured enthusiast who has the power to make people feel that religion is release and joy. Too many of us have well-nigh forgotten that Christianity is "good, mery, glad and joyful tydings, that maketh a mannes hert glad, and maketh hym synge, daunce and leepe for joye," as William Tyndale put it in his prologue to the New Testament of the year 1525. The spark can go out so easily and the fire will disappear.

Horowitz, one of the world's greatest pianists, was known always for the perfection of his technique. Just twenty-five years after his first concert at Carnegie Hall in New York, he returned to play the same Tchaikovsky concerto at the same place with the same orchestra. Interestingly enough, his music was discussed by Olin Downes, the same critic who had reviewed his performance twenty-five years before. And comparing the two concerts, Olin Downes said that Horowitz after a quarter of a century had become gigantic, unpolished, imprudent, overwhelming. Was he not saying that the musician had found something even more wonderful than perfection of execution? The music had captured his spirit. This can happen to a preacher when the fire of the good news of redemption rages in his heart. And it has

[12] Macmillan, 1949, 9.

a power that the most perfectly delivered discourse never knows.

Routine can win its final victory over us, unless we have from time to time the soul-stirring experience of conversions. One of my friends some time ago greeted me with a new light in his eyes as he told me about a wonderful experience. A young man engaged to a girl in his church had deserted her just the day before the wedding. Finally he crept back shamefacedly and had come to this minister to confess his dissolute life. When that young man knelt in that study, he found something he never discovered before. A week later the marriage took place and when the young couple had dedicated their home to God, my friend said that this had restored something to his ministry that he had not realized had gone from it. "Why," said he, "this ought to happen all the time." So it had, and so it may. We must not forget St. Paul's promise to every preacher: "All this is from God, who through Christ reconciled us to himself and gave us the ministry of reconciliation. . . ." (II Corinthians 5:18).

We miss our opportunities because we do not see them until too late. Molière shows an impressive consultation, with a group of doctors breaking up and a questioner asking one of them where they were going. One of the doctors answered solemnly that they were off to see a man who had died the day before in order to learn what should have been done to prevent his death.[13] Christian preachers need to get out of the category of postmortem experts and enter into their true heritage as messengers of life, for we serve One who is not the God of the dead but the God of the living.

[13] Cailliet, *The Christian Approach to Culture,* Abingdon, 1953, 264.

Listen to this tribute which Dorothy Sayers has paid to G. K. Chesterton:

> To the young people of my generation, G. K. C. was a kind of Christian liberator. Like a benificent bomb, he blew out of the Church a quantity of stained glass of a very poor period, and let in gusts of fresh air, in which the dead leaves of doctrine danced with all the energy of Our Lady's tumbler. . . .
>
> It was . . . stimulating to be told that Christianity was not a dull thing but a gay thing, not a stick-in-the-mud thing but an adventurous thing, not an unintelligent thing but a wise thing, and indeed a shrewd thing—for while it was still frequently admitted to be harmless as the dove, it had almost ceased to be credited with the wisdom of the serpent. Above all, it was refreshing to see Christian polemic conducted with offensive rather than defensive weapons.[14]

What that great master of paradox did for Miss Sayers and many others of his generation and ours, the Christian preacher ought to be doing for the blasé and weary worshipers in the congregation. But this change cannot take place until we understand that the message we proclaim is one of breaking up and building, of shaking to pieces and re-establishing, of giving a secure home base and a dangerous trail to follow. In a word, it is a message of what a man's life may become if God has his chance at it.

The message of redemption cannot be preached except in terms of love, and the 13th chapter of I Corinthians is one which ought to be read often and carefully by every preacher. We must believe that the love of Christ manifested in our own poor lives can work miracles in other men's lives. One of our great dangers lies in becoming too sophisticated and too self-centered to believe that the lively

[14] Preface to *The Surprise* by G. K. Chesterton, Sheed & Ward.

word of God can redeem. The great reward of our ministry will not lie in particular honors which may come to us, though this may be the experience of many. It will not consist in salaries or positions to which we may be elected by our brethren. It is rather in the changed life of some person who found redemption through our words and our ministry. It is not in the places of power which come to some administrators but in being close to the disease of the world with an awareness of a healing power to restore health, that we find the real reward of life.

I shall never forget a Japanese man stopping me on the street of the little town of Lahaina on the island of Maui because he recognized me from a picture in a college annual of Nebraska Wesleyan University. He stopped to tell how much he appreciated what I had done for his son, who in the difficult days of the war had found his faith strengthened and his courage maintained through some poor unconscious efforts of my own. Other men in other walks of life may have their high moments and their times of triumph, but none of them, I am convinced, can compare with that wonderful moment in the life of the preacher when someone tells him that he was the instrument God used to bring the saving grace of Christ to another person.

There is a letter which John Wesley wrote to Francis Asbury on September 20, 1788. I look at it from time to time for my soul's sake and I share it with you, though its precise implication may not fit you as it does me. John Wesley wrote:

> But in one point, my dear Brother, I am a little afraid the Doctor [Coke] and you differ from me. I study to be little, you study to be great; I creep, you strut along; I found a school, you a col-

lege—nay, and call it after your own names! Oh beware! Do not seek to be something! Let me be nothing, and Christ be all in all.

One instance of this, your greatness, has given me great concern. How can you—how dare you suffer yourself to be called a Bishop! I shudder—I start at the very thought. Men may call me a knave, or a fool, a rascal, a scoundrel, and I am content, but they shall never, by my consent, call me a Bishop! For my sake—for Christ's sake, put a full end to this! . . . Thus, my dear Frankie, I have told you all that is in my heart. . . .

What that great evangelist was doing essentially, I think, was warning that when a man in the ministry begins to desire anything else except evangelistic success, he is on the wrong track. Other things will come in and become substitutes for conversions. We ought to share that concern, for once we begin to neglect our function as the proclaimers of the good news of redemption the power goes out of our words and joy leaves our hearts. What a tremendous thing it is to know that we are ordained to preach a message which may send people forth from the church different from when they came, and give them grace, faith, freedom, or as the New Testament puts it so simply, salvation.

VII *Good News of Truth*

> Therefore I intend always to remind you of these things, though you know them and are established in the truth that you have. II PETER 1:12

Ivor Brown, drama critic for the London *Observer* and a prominent figure in the English literary scene for more than thirty years, wrote a description of the Christmas season in London and among other things commented on Christmas churchgoing. Admitting that he is not a churchman, he goes on to give his reactions to the number of Englishmen who use the church for special occasions and have no time for it at any other season. How is it possible, he wonders, to admit the validity of the sacred mysteries one or two days a year and then ignore them completely the rest of the year? Part of the fault, he believes, lies with the churches. He writes:

> During a recent Christmas I received from my local parish church an invitation which struck me as really lamentable in its tone:
>
> Christmas Day is the birthday of our Lord Jesus Christ

—Will you let him share it with you at one or more of these services?

Will I let Him? Should not I be told firmly and even fiercely, that, if I believe in the facts of the Christian story, then it is a supreme privilege to be allowed to share in this grandeur of spiritual opportunity, and that I am committing unpardonable folly if I miss the chance at sharing such communion.[1]

What this literary man has felt apparently makes too little impression upon preachers. Instead of being men with something to offer of ultimate worth, we act like mendicants begging for a handout. We seem to have lost all sense of the Truth and we have no clear certainty of the ultimate authority to which we owe unqualified allegiance. I have observed ministers and churches degrade themselves to the point of granting immediately whatever the secular world asks for, lest they offend someone. Announcements will be made and the activities of other organizations will be promoted on Sunday morning as if the church existed primarily as a propaganda agency for more important institutions and programs. This tendency has been carried so far among us that I have heard parents get very angry if a local church intimated that they must take some responsibility if they expected the church to accept their children in an already overcrowded Sunday School. Is it possible that one of the things which we have forgotten is that we proclaim the good news of truth, and that truth is not apologized for but proclaimed.

Protestants have been more guilty of this tendency than Catholics. However, one of my friends reports that in a Catholic church in Chicago he found this announcement

[1] Brown, *Saturday Review,* Nov. 20, 1952, 7.

concerning a certain Saturday in January: "The Blessed Virgin of Fatima will be waiting for you this coming Saturday, don't let her down." This may bring us some small comfort, but on the whole we must confess that our Catholic brethren have a great deal to teach us concerning the attitude of an institution which claims to be nothing less than the revelation and proclaimer of the truth of God.

There has grown up among us a class of people whose religion consists for the most part in being open-minded about everything and convinced about nothing. A man once referred to them as people who sow their wild oats during the week, then go to church once in a while and pray halfheartedly for a crop failure. The vain pretensions of this class of twilight Christians have been shrewdly analyzed by Alice Meynell in her poem, "The Newer Vainglory":

> For I am tolerant, generous, keep no rules,
> And the age honors me.
> Thank God, I am not as these rigid fools,
> Even as this Pharisee.[2]

A generation that has tried to live within the framework of relativism is frightened to death of the idea that there may be absolute truths which can neither be dodged nor manipulated. Winston Churchill once remarked that men occasionally stumble over the truth but most of them pick themselves up and hurry off as if nothing had happened. They hurry off because they are afraid to consider the implications for themselves. It is so much more comfortable to believe that nothing has final significance and everything

[2] Used by permission of Burns, Oates & Washborne, Ltd. and Wilfred Meynell, executor.

can be arranged according to the pattern we have chosen. The men who wrote the New Testament were not of that opinion.

The later letters of the New Testament are regarded generally by scholars as being of smaller stature than the Gospels and the Letters of Paul. This is not to say that there are lacking great passages and profound insights. But most of the later epistles do not manifest the genius and revelation that one feels in the more original writings of the New Testament. Probably they do not constitute the books which feed our spirits most adequately.

But there is one element in these later letters which is very important for us to observe and consider. It is the assumption that something has happened which provides a criterion for judgment of all of life. It is a faith that truth came into the world and that men need never again grope among lies and half-truths. It is a feeling, not often expressed directly, that men now have a foundation to stand upon, a guide to direct them, and a standard by which human desires and behavior can be measured. That spirit finds expression in the Fourth Gospel in these words: "For the law was given through Moses; grace and truth came through Jesus Christ" (John 1:17).

Not all of us will deserve places with the apostles and the prophets. Much of our work will be bearing witness to a revelation that came to greater men than ourselves. But no Christian minister ought to lack this fundamental confidence that his message is grounded in truth that has been tested and tried but never shaken. We do not offer men one good product among many. We do not tell them that we should like to have them try this way of life and see how it pleases them. There is a sense in which we too proclaim in this generation, "Beloved, being very eager to write to you of our common salvation, I found it necessary to write appealing to you to contend for the faith which was once for all delivered to the saints" (Jude 3). We will not contend for a static faith which can be frozen, but we do proclaim a living faith in a living Person which at a particular time came into human experience to guide us into all knowledge necessary for understanding the destiny God has ordained for us.

1. MEASUREMENT

But be doers of the word. . . . JAMES 1:22

One of the great difficulties of human life is to take an objective point of view regarding our activities. Most of what we do is dictated by the environment in which we live. We find ourselves doing a number of things which thoughtlessly we have assumed to be important simply because these things are being done. It is disturbing to contemplate how many men have never sought to measure their living, nor have they ever stopped to ask whether life as they live it has anything more than passing significance. It is true that there are large numbers of people who are no longer able to judge realistically concerning themselves. They will never know how to begin their measurement unless someone comes to their aid.

The great awakening for many a man comes when it is revealed to him that most of the things for which he has given his life are really tawdry. I have talked with a number of men who confessed that a long illness provided the opportunity for their first real look at themselves. When Jefferson Selleck, the hero of a recent best-selling novel, had a heart attack and stood at the very edge of the abyss, he was told by his doctor that now he must grow up. He came to the realization that for the first time he was facing the question of what his life had meant, if anything, and what significance it had achieved, if any. He is the man of our time and the man to whom we preach.

One of the main reasons that men fear a real experience of God is a kind of instinctive certainty that such an experience will reveal most of their lives as pretense. To get too close to Him, who is the center of things and the ground of their being, will make them look at themselves through His eyes, and that is more than most men dare risk. Emil Brunner has observed this human truth and translated it into what he calls "The Law of the Closeness of Relation." He puts it down in these words:

> The nearer anything lies to that center of existence where we are concerned with the whole, that is, with man's relation to God and the being of the Person, the greater is the disturbance of rational knowledge by sin; the farther away anything lies from this center, the less is the disturbance felt, and the less difference is there between knowing as a believer or an unbeliever. This disturbance reaches its maximum in theology and its minimum in the exact sciences, and zero in the sphere of the formal.[3]

Which is to say, we need not expect men gladly to seek the truth until the lies have become unbearable, as indeed one day they must. But the preacher's opportunity and responsibility lies in bringing to bear upon human activity the measurement of the truth of Jesus Christ. For as men come closer to him, the more impossible it is to escape the disturbing knowledge of their sin and littleness. The Gospel with ruthless directness makes us understand that some of

[3] Brunner, *Revelation and Reason,* Westminster, 1946, 383.

these trinkets which we have valued are actually worthless, and that in their pursuit we have missed the real treasures of human experience because a foolish generation has pasted cheap labels on them.

The danger of course is that the one who proclaims the word shall become contaminated with the falsity of his time. He may lose his moral judgment, and finally the slow stain of the world colors his own life. Perhaps no generation of preachers has faced greater temptations in this realm than our own. Over against the blurred and sentimental judgments of our time, it is for us to hold the sharp, incisive insights of the New Testament.

There is no safety for us unless we have a dependable measurement. One of the easiest things in the world is to adjust ourselves to small things and imagine that they are big. The great temptation of humanity is to get used to things which ought constantly to shock us and disturb us. If we should compare the kind of behavior which no longer keeps us from sleeping at night with the behavior which our fathers attacked with all their vigor, we would realize how the trend has been in the direction of believing that monstrous things are now necessary and therefore right.

But what happens to an age is the reflection of what is happening to the individual citizens of that period. One of the irreducible tensions of life is trying to decide whether one is compromising things which ought not to be compromised or whether one is growing more mature. Our only safety is to have some opportunity to enter into the presence often of the One who knows the answers to these questions and whose spirit can guide us into all truth. The need is for an absolute and the Christian faith is an affirmation that in Jesus Christ it has been given to us. J. B. Priestly, the English novelist, spent a winter on the Arizona desert and wrote with great eloquence concerning the Grand Canyon. Though carved out by the Colorado River, he was certain that God gave that river its instructions. Then he remarked that if he were an American he would judge everything in the light of the Canyon. He would ask whether a certain politician or a certain policy was worthy of a country that had in it the Grand Canyon of the Colorado. So God has given men Jesus, that they might ask at all times how this thing looks in the light of his teaching; what is the size of this impulse and this program when measured by his perfect life. And while it is true that men flee from him because of the terrible contrast they see in their own strivings when compared with his greatness, nevertheless they are also drawn to him beyond their power to resist. He becomes at once the spiritual magnet of the race as well as the judgment which shames and frightens us.

All of our measurements are so partial and inadequate. G. K. Chesterton one time remarked that Omar Khayyám lived in the basement and thought it was the whole house. Well, we are always doing that, and most of our trouble lies in assuming that partial insight is complete vision. The Christians through the centuries have discovered that in Jesus they have the whole picture, the whole measurement. Which is another way of saying that they discover in him the truth, and we preach the Christ whose example and presence sheds adequate light on all our problems.

2. DIRECTION

But according to his promise we wait for new heavens and a new earth in which righteousness dwells. II PETER 3:13

Perhaps there is no better news for a groping generation

than the good news of guidance. It is not necessary that men should be rich or live in luxury to be happy. It is not necessary that a nation should have achieved final success in the realm of economics. But because we are men, it is necessary that we should have some idea of where we are going or at least some concept of where we ought to go, if we are to live. A young chaplain who had served in the Korean War told me that the hardest thing of all was not the cold nor the danger but the wonder on the part of the men as to what it was all about and what would be accomplished in the end. No matter how difficult the way may be, if we can be sure that the way leads to light, we will find the strength and courage to follow it. But if our choices have been wrong and we circle back to where we began, then panic seizes us. Bernard Berenson wrote:

> When does decline of a ruling nation or of a ruling class within a nation set in? Perhaps when it begins to parry challenges with palliatives, and worse still with a pretense of ignoring them.[4]

This is another way of saying that when we lose the sense of direction, our decline has begun.

The loss of direction is one of the most subtle and common experiences in human life. It is so easy to veer a little too much to the left or to the right and discover after the years have passed by that one has been wandering around in the woods and making no progress toward a desired destination. For sometimes a man wakes up at the bottom of an abyss over which he has tumbled and all the time he thought he was following a safe road. Most people do not deliberately choose the wrong way and most of them were

[4] Berenson, *op. cit.*, 87.

unaware of what was happening to them until it was too late.

Generally, the men who lose their direction do not go over a cliff in a spectacular crash, nor do they come suddenly to the obvious dead end. They usually experience what is in some ways a more horrible fate, namely, the realization that they have wandered far and traveled hard, but they are doomed to end but a little way from where they began. This is the most horrible awakening that comes to people because they never can escape the feeling that life ought to progress. The humiliating realization that a man's life has moved nowhere in particular means that his existence has ended in an inglorious failure. Men can endure all kinds of suffering and make innumerable sacrifices if they believe that they are advancing in the right direction. But if at long last their life seems to have been merely a confusion and a betrayal, then hope dies and despair is ultimate.

This loss of direction has been the characteristic disappointment of our generation. It has been a very great disillusionment to many an intelligent man that his lust for success was no proper guide for him to follow. At the basis of the anxiety of Western civilization today there is a growing certainty that the paths of science and materialism have not and cannot take us to a satisfying human destination.

In the later letters of the New Testament there is a great concern with false teachers and false prophets. Those writers felt it necessary to warn contemporary Christians that men professing to be true spokesmen for Christ were among them, misleading them, and misdirecting them. They were experiencing then, as we have been experiencing in our time, how easy it is to follow after men with high promises described in pious phraseology, but whose spirits are contrary to our Lord. Trading on the human desire to find an easier way if possible, these are the individuals who win a following through their false promises. If there seems to be an inordinate amount of going back to something which has already happened in the late Epistles, it is because they are aware that if there are false guides there is also a true Guide who still will direct men even as he did the Twelve who walked with him. A description of a U. S. jet plane, the Douglas Skynight, says that it "is equipped with a radar system that locks the plane onto the target in the dark." The men who wrote the later letters of the New Testament felt that Jesus Christ did that for them.

Let it be said again and again that the men who lose the way do not deliberately choose the wrong and follow the wrong sign. They are nearly always well-meaning individuals who would like to chip off some of the rough corners of truth and make it roll. They have been tempted to believe that truth can be manipulated and used instead of standing foursquare at every crossroad, pointing to the straight and narrow way.

It has not been the Christian experience that the Christian faith is a set of precise directions available for every minute decision. Those who insist that it is, conveniently forget the places where their guidance was either absent or mistaken. It has been popular to assume that the road becomes plain and the decision becomes clear if a man yields himself completely to Christ. I have heard testimonies to the effect that even the most inconsequential decisions can never go wrong if one has the right spirit. Such an attitude falls into the same category as the use of the sacred lot, and the church has never been willing to proclaim that the

Christian could be certain that no wrong decision would be made and no wrong turning taken.

But the good news of the Gospel is that we will have guidance for the next step even when we cannot see too far into the future. Jesus warned his followers that they should not try to live far ahead, but be content with the day itself. It is not true that the golden rule is the whole of religion, but it is true that the golden rule is a very dependable guide so far as our personal relationships are concerned. It is our lack of imagination that leads us into so much trouble with others, and the golden rule helps to put us in the other man's place before we act or speak. A friend of mind told me that a business executive went to see the play *Death of a Salesman,* which tells of the pathetic loneliness, the firing, and the final suicide of a traveling salesman. The employer went to the phone immediately at the close of the play, called his office manager, and told him to withhold the dismissal notice which was to be given to one of the older employees the next day. It took a drama to make this man enter into the experience of another man. There is a sense in which the golden rule keeps us ever crossing beyond the boundaries of our own persons into the lives of others. Because our personal relationships represent the fundamental things in our lives and the foundations upon which everything else has to rest, this is guidance indeed.

Men who walk close to Jesus have been aware that in dark times they could usually tell what the next decision ought to be. Let us not forget the New Testament testimony that things went right with people as long as they stayed in the presence of Jesus. The difficulties began when they followed afar off or when they left the boundaries of his influence. And no rule, whether it be golden or otherwise, ever suffices as an adequate guide unless it can lead us into the presence of our Lord.

A great deal of interest was aroused by Gandhi's day of silence. It came to have mystical, Oriental meaning, and seemed to symbolize a spiritual genius whose life was far away from the practical everyday existence of the men of the West. Yet he says that at the beginning he needed a day off and a time to be by himself, so he clothed it with other meanings and other reasons. But as he said in his honest and direct way, at the beginning he just wanted a day to himself. Put in this light, it is not the symbol of something far removed from our own needs and desires. One of the things Christianity does for us is to help us to be alone and not get bored. When we can be apart for a time with Him, enough light falls on the path to make the next step clear.

But our good news of direction is also that we can have the long look which gives us the vision of the new heaven and the new earth. Immediate decision is to be made not only in the light of the immediate problem but in the faith that truth must conquer and Jesus Christ must reign everywhere. This is the Christian interpretation of history and it is the Christian faith describing the future.

A nation is tempted to believe that God dozes and men can hurry through the accomplishment of their own will before He awakens. The church is tempted to believe that just at this particular time He may be looking the other way, so we can cut through the forbidden territory and come out on the right path down below. A man hopes that God may be very busy about other things and overlook him now for a little while, that he may follow this interesting sidepath and be back again before he is missed. But our good news is that God does not cease His reigning at any moment and if we keep our eye on that heaven and earth wherein dwelleth righteousness, we shall know the direction we shall have to go.

Not the least of our clues for the choosing of the right direction is the experience of our immortality, which not only holds before our eyes a future bliss, but touches every present experience with its benediction. We become aware that some things are false for immortal creatures and some things are true. We learn that there is a direction which a passing animal might take but not an eternal spirit. Even in the valley of the shadow of death we are promised that we shall walk through it and come out safely at the other end. Men always take the wrong turning when they forget this truth about themselves. But when eternal life is a present joy, so much darkness on the road suddenly disappears. Albert Schweitzer wrote something back in 1933 that brings great comfort to me twenty years later:

> . . . The spiritual and material misery to which mankind of today is delivering itself through its renunciation of thinking and of the ideals which spring therefrom, I picture to myself in its utmost compass. And yet I remain optimistic. One belief of my childhood I have preserved with the certainty that I can never lose it: belief in truth. I am confident that the spirit generated by truth is stronger than the force of circumstances. In my view no other destiny awaits mankind than that which, through its mental and spiritual disposition, it prepares for itself. Therefore I do not believe that it will have to tread the road to ruin to the end.
>
> If men can be found who revolt against the spirit of thoughtlessness, and who are personalities sound enough and profound enough to let the ideals of ethical progress radiate from them as a force, there will start an activity of the spirit which will be

strong enough to evoke a new mental and spiritual disposition in mankind.

Because I have confidence in the power of truth and of the spirit, I believe in the future of mankind.[5]

This, it seems to me, is a great affirmation of confidence in the possibility of Christian men finding the road again for themselves and for their generation.

3. FINALITY

Jesus Christ is the same yesterday and today and forever. HEBREWS 13:8

A most significant word concerning the resurrection of Jesus has been given to us by Henry Sloane Coffin:

Resurrection does not mean escape from this tough earth into a more favorable realm. Such a flight would have been for Jesus loss of the battle into which He had thrown His all. Resurrection means return in power, despite death and burial, and going on with divine force in and through His Church, His Body. Easter is the festival of the trustworthiness of God for those who confide in Him.[6]

When we talk about the finality of Jesus Christ we are not talking about something limited, but about his revelation of the essential trustworthiness and unchanging power of the Almighty. The temptation to make of our religion a closed system which can be contained in a closed mind is ever with us. Always we are in hopes that some last word has been spoken which makes no further thinking necessary. Men seem to be more tempted to seek this solution in religion than in any other field, although it is certainly not

[5] Schweitzer, *Out of My Life and Thought,* Holt, 1933, Epilogue.
[6] Coffin, *op. cit.,* 54.

lacking in any of the significant realms of human life. What may be called the fundamentalist's mentality is not only a religious tragedy, for it appears in politics, economics, art, and science. It is the fear of growth and the suspicion of change.

In a living society controversy is the lifeblood. "A university that is not controversial is not a university," as Robert M. Hutchins has said. Only totalitarianism and death demand an end to the discussion of the vital issues. If there is not a "great debate" going on among a people, something is wrong and they should be seriously concerned. Let us learn once and for all that when there is lively discussion and difference of opinion, we are not in the presence of weakness but of strength.

An attitude of dull acquiescence is of danger to any community, to any communion, and to any society. A corpse can be embalmed and kept in a fair state of preservation for a long time, as the Russians have discovered in the case of Lenin. But the worship of a corpse is always idolatry and it leads finally to excesses and madness. Worship must be centered in something that is alive. There are too many Christians who read the New Testament clear up to the Crucifixion and then apparently close the book before they read about the Resurrection. There are any number of people who revel in the birth stories of Jesus, especially at Christmas time, but never adjust themselves to the fact that the baby became a man and a prophet.

When Jesus came down from the Mount of Transfiguration he discovered a great crowd gathered. When he inquired what the discussion was about, a man replied that he had brought his sick boy to the disciples and they could not heal him. Remember how the father described the case, then closed with these words: "'But if you can do anything, have pity on us and help us.' And Jesus said to him, 'If you can! All things are possible to him who believes.' Immediately the father of the child cried out and said, 'I believe; help my unbelief!'" (Mark 9:22–24). Can a man believe and not believe at the same time? It is the Christian experience that the believer stands in the position of assurance and at the same time is engaged in a continual struggle for faith. There is a final assurance which a man holds and there is also the struggle to appropriate and take hold of faith as he faces this particular problem. It is the application of this finality to the immediate that represents the growing edge of Christian experience. It is as if a man said to himself that he knows this is ultimately true but dare he believe that it is immediately possible. So at long last the strange paradox of assurance and uncertainty is solved when a man recognizes that the finality has to become immediately experienced.

There comes a time to the seeking Christian when he may affirm that he knows in whom he believes. He accepts forevermore the proposition that Jesus was right and that in Christianity we have the revelation of the ultimate truths of God. When that happens, this is the end of the warfare in his mind between his religion and his science or between his ethics and nature. Any fear that there may come along some new discovery which will upset his faith or his theology has now been banished. The quarreling with every differing person comes to an end. Strangely enough instead of demanding uniformity, he begins to seek and discover the unity in the midst of differences. True tolerance is born because faith in Jesus as the final truth brings patience and sympathy and love.

One of the most amazing things about Jesus is his ability to see nobility where others could not see it, and recognize virtue where it was unobservable by the community. The disciples might become upset because some other teacher did things differently from the way they were taught to do them. But their Master, far from being upset, was glad to welcome any individual whose approach might differ if his seeking was honest. He never bound his followers in any straight jacket of behavior or belief. The disciples did not find themselves forced into any common mold such as the totalitarians desire for their followers. But each man had his own personality sharpened and enriched. Having come to a common acceptance of the Galilean as the Messiah, they found that their individualities were even more respected than before. The acceptance of Jesus Christ as the revelation of a final truth accentuates the significance of personality and never forces men into a set pattern.

There is an incident in Greek mythology which gives us light on the Christian experience of Jesus. One man asks another: "O Iole, how did you know that Hercules was a god?" And Iole answers: "Because I was content the moment my eyes fell on him. When I beheld Theseus, I desired that I might see him offer battle, or at least guide his horses in the chariot race; but Hercules did not wait for a contest; he conquered whether he stood, or walked, or sat, or whatever he did." So men have bowed before the One who was the way, the truth, and the life, whenever they came into his presence.

Great teachers can hardly escape the temptation to stamp their personalities upon their students. It is not always a deliberate desire or a conscious ambition to send out into the world replicas of themselves. But if a man has a particular system or method which he believes to be the best, he becomes an evangelist with so much power that students are sometimes overwhelmed. How many minor incarnations of John Dewey we have observed in our time, and how often we can tell who taught the young preacher his homiletics by listening to him preach just once. There are not too many teachers like Dr. Jowett of Balliol College, of whom it was said that he sent out more students unlike himself than any professor at Oxford.

But the great teacher who truly educates does what the word means literally—he draws out. He vitalizes every individual power and stimulates every talent but he never seeks to confine those powers or talents within a framework which he has forged. So when we come to recognize that in Jesus Christ there is a fine truth to which all other truths must be related, we do not fear authoritarianism or a tyranny over the minds and spirits of men. The New Testament is not concerned because the false teachers are different but because these men are seeking to substitute passing notions for an absolute finality. Jesus Christ who is always the same is also the one who visits us continually with the great divine surprise.

4. FOR THE PREACHER

I John am he who heard and saw these things. REVELATION 22:8

Once we have accepted the Christian Gospel as ultimate truth, then we are in position to speak our prophetic words and pronounce our judgments on the contemporary scene. That which may pass the notice of most observers and may be overlooked by men whose concern is with profit and loss will stand revealed to the Christian preacher in true outline when the Gospel truth shines upon it. From the days of

Amos it has been the men who knew God who also knew society and its diseases. When it was obvious to men that stealing was wrong, but not so obvious that stealing could be done through respectable methods, Washington Gladden at Yale in 1877 said:

> The friendless poor get short shrift and summary vengeance; the rich rascal can secure delays and perversions of equity and often go scot-free. The man who steals a ham from a freight car goes to jail; the man who steals the railroad goes to the United States Senate.[7]

When all of life is brought into the searching criticisms of the Gospel's truth, it is amazing how all that is false and evil becomes so apparent.

It is this Gospel truth that reveals the emptiness of so much of our political oratory and popular superstitions. It was William MacAdoo who commented on the speeches of a certain American president as leaving "the impression of an army of pompous phrases moving over a landscape in search of an idea." The search, he added, was ever futile.[8] The cheap triviality and vulgar popularity of so many after-dinner speakers are unnoticed by the widely unread men who attend the meeting. But the Christian can never escape a sense of the essential tawdriness which shines through the clever stories and the little tricks the speaker has developed. The public can be fooled and people can be easily misled because the lie can be made to appear to be the truth and the wide road can be interpreted as the straight path. The Christian preacher convinced of the final truth of his message has the criterion by which he judges the spurious claims and impossible promises of the lying teachers and the false prophets.

[7] Jones, *The Royalty of the Pulpit,* 151.

[8] Holbrook, *Lost Men of American History,* Macmillan, 1946, 329.

It is the Christian Gospel that can declare the nature of the foundation upon which men must stand. For it is Christianity that knows the truth about men, about all men, and it sees in humanity that there is a common seeking and a common need. Rousseau can shout hysterically that he is different from other men, but John Donne speaks the truth of Christ when he confesses that he is a part of mankind and the bell always tolls for him. So in a time when we are tempted to say this is for us but not for them, or this is the way we are but they are not, the good news of the Gospel tells us that we are all sons of the Father and that in reality our life is a common one.

The lack of authority in the modern pulpit is one of its most unlovely characteristics. Yet if we long for a bygone day when the preacher spoke his word and people had to accept it or else lose their social status, we would do well to remember that men never have power like that without abusing it. The Inquisition was not the work of sinners but of sincere though fanatical Christian men. Convinced that they were doing the work of the church, they could find reason to use atrocious cruelty in silencing heresy and in putting down rebellion. It is certainly a sobering thought to realize that the barbaric methods of our police states have been modeled after methods used by churchmen in days gone by. Strangely enough, an authority that killed whom it would and silenced the one with whom it disagreed did not accomplish any lasting triumph. The church was not strengthened thereby, and if one argues that the Reformation was hindered by these methods, it could also be argued that it was made inevitable by them.

The authority of the preacher has to be the authority of truth. If he can believe that the good news which he preaches is true and by his manner proclaim to his people that because it is true he puts before them the issues of life and death, then his authority will be real. We talk too much in our pulpits as if what we were saying is interesting, we hope, and of some intellectual significance. We talk too little as if what we were saying was based on the very word of God. John Bunyan one time said, "Of all temptations I ever met with in life, to question the truth of His Gospel is the worst, and the worst to be borne." To that I can say Amen, and perhaps many another preacher has had to learn from bitter suffering what Bunyan means.

Many of us have come out of our seminary experience so filled with questions about the religion of our boyhood and so overwhelmed with what we have learned about comparative religion, that we would much rather be called upon to define what we do not believe and why, than proclaim what we do believe with all our hearts. I do not think there is any way out of this and it is a price which a man has to pay for clearing up the fuzziness of his mind. But soon or late the time must come when the Gospel bursts upon him with the assurance that it is true. He knows in that moment that while there are many questions he will ask and a great deal of new light to be expected, still in the Christian faith he has the truth. His message has been given to him and His authority has been bestowed upon him. It may come very suddenly or it may take a long time. It may creep into his consciousness so gradually that one day he realizes it is there, but when it first entered he cannot tell; or it may come to him with the suddenness of a conversion. But come it must if he is to preach. Once this has happened to him, a man must pray that any gifts God has given to him will be dedicated to the one final goal of preaching the Gospel as the truth of God.

Once a man has this authority, it will give him added effectiveness and also added temptation. Aldous Huxley has analyzed this as clearly as any man when he writes:

> To Urbain Grandier, for example, the Good Fairy had brought, along with solid talents, the most dazzling of all gifts, and the most dangerous—eloquence. Spoken by a good actor—and every great preacher, every successful advocate a politician is, among other things, a consummate actor—words can exercise an almost magical power, even the best-intentioned of public speakers probably do more harm than good. When an orator, by the mere magic of words and a golden voice, persuades his audience of the rightness of a bad cause, we are very properly shocked. We ought to feel the same dismay whenever we find the same irrelevant tricks being used to persuade people of the rightness of a good cause. The belief engendered may be desirable, but the grounds for it are intrinsically wrong, and those who use the devices of oratory for instilling even right beliefs are guilty of pandering to the least creditable elements in human nature. By exercising their disastrous gift of the gab, they deepen the quasi-hypnotic trance in which most human beings live and from which it is the aim and purpose of all true philosophy, all genuinely spiritual religion to deliver them. Moreover, there cannot be effective oratory without over-simplification. But you cannot over-simplify without distorting the facts. Even when he is doing his best to tell the truth, the successful orator is ipso facto a liar. And most successful orators, it is hardly necessary to add, are not even trying to tell the truth; they are trying to evoke sympathy for their friends and antipathy for their opponents.[9]

This is a hard word but a necessary one, for it tells us that we are all under extreme danger and judgment at all times. It makes us aware that for men it is not possible to speak the truth, and nothing but the truth, unless God performs

[9] Huxley, *op. cit.*, 18.

the miracle for them. But to be aware of the danger offers the hope that we shall pray for and receive protection and cleansing.

Truth is found in a life and it is the genius of our faith that it does not try to sum truth up in a definition or to make a proposition out of it which we can use for propaganda purposes. It insists, on the contrary, that the truth is in Jesus. That means that the truth must be in us, and the final authority for our truth will be in the life which we live. It is not a matter of complete consistency or logic. It is a matter of the good will of love and the pure heart. It was found supremely in a Person and it comes to men through other persons. Through the preacher truth with its living quality springs out of the Book and men feel as they did when on the hillside a Teacher opened his mouth and taught them.

In the third century B.C. Archimedes, a Greek mathematician, made a statement which has been quoted many times: "Give me a lever long enough, and a fulcrum strong enough, and single-handed I can move the world." It is the typical word of a man who sees the world in terms of a physical mass, and it has been the popular idea of a world whose gods have been material might and energy. But Joseph Conrad answered the Greek mathematician by saying, "Don't talk to me of your Archimedes level . . . but give me the right word and the right accent and I will move the world." It is not the right argument, not the right formula, not the right equation that we seek now. It is the right word and accent. There was such a Word which became flesh, and it was grace and truth. If it has become the lost word of our time, it is for us to find the accent which will convince men of its authority and power.

Set in Linotype Granjon
Format by Edwin H. Kaplin
Manufactured by The Haddon Craftsmen, Inc.
Published by HARPER & BROTHERS, *New York*